CULTURE OF EXCELLENCE

What We Can Learn From The Yankees About Leadership

CULTURE OF EXCELLENCE

What We Can Learn From The Yankees About Leadership

COLIN CERNIGLIA

Talent 409 Publishing
Charlotte, NC

TALENT 409
LEADERSHIP ACADEMY

Colin Cerniglia
P.O. Box 217094
Charlotte, NC 28221-7094
colin@talent409.com

ISBN: 978-0-578-71037-2
Library of Congress Control Number: 2020910817
1st Edition
Cover design by MIBLART

For my wife, Christine,
who believed in this writing just as much as I did.

To my parents, John and Maureen,
for your unconditional love and support.

To my daughter, Stella,
this book is my first gift to you.

For all of the Yankee fans and for the people
who want to become better leaders,
this work is especially for you.

CONTENTS

Introduction

The Bronx Zoo and Birth of a Model Organization.............................. xiii
    1989...xiii
    Why the Yankees?...xv
    What Is There to Be Discovered?................................. xvii

PILLAR ONE

LEADERSHIP.. xix

Chapter One

The Boss ....- 1 -
    Who Is the Boss?...- 1 -
    A Brief History Lesson About the Yankees.....................- 3 -
    Steinbrenner's Vision for Excellence (1973–1990)......................- 4 -
    Steinbrenner's Leadership Profile ....- 7 -
    Leading with Empathy ....- 9 -
    The End of Steinbrenner's "First Term" as Owner ....- 13 -
    The Start of Steinbrenner's
    "Second Term" as Owner (1993–2010)..- 16 -
    Summary of *The Boss* ....- 17 -

Chapter Two

The Manager's Seat ....- 19 -
    Building a New Foundation: Life Without the Boss ....- 21 -
    The Birth of the Joe Torre Era ....- 23 -
    Building Trust...- 27 -
    Establishing a Working Relationship with a Difficult Boss........- 32 -
    The Transition of Joes: From Torre to Girardi......................- 33 -
    Displaying Accountability...- 36 -
    Treating People with Respect......................................- 37 -
    Making Difficult Decisions...- 38 -
    Yankees History Lesson: 2013–2017 ....- 40 -

Failure to Communicate .... - 43 -
Now Managing for the Yankees, Aaron "Bleeping" Boone........ - 44 -
Summary of *The Manager's Seat*............................ - 49 -

Chapter Three

Evil Empire Architects.. - 51 -
Yankees Overview: 1984–1998 .... - 52 -
Being Bold: The Start of the Brian Cashman Era .... - 55 -
Understanding Internal Development................................ - 58 -
Being Unafraid to Have Difficult Conversations .... - 60 -
Supplementing Internal Development
with Outside Reinforcements .... - 62 -
Hal Steinbrenner: A Forward Way of Doing Business .... - 65 -
Summary of *Evil Empire Architects*................................ - 69 -
KEY POINTS: LEADERSHIP .... - 71 -

PILLAR TWO

CULTURE–PEOPLE AND COMMUNITY... - 73 -

Chapter Four

Culture .... - 75 -
A Lesson in Organizational Dysfunction............................. - 77 -
Emerging Leaders... - 79 -
It Feels Like Home.. - 82 -
Blending Unique Personalities....................................... - 84 -
Frailty of Human Life... - 88 -
Summary of *Culture* .... - 92 -

Chapter Five

Player-Led Teams .... - 93 -
David Cone: Leader, But Not Captain................................ - 94 -
The Captain, Part I: Don Mattingly.................................. - 99 -
The Captain, Part II: Derek Jeter.................................... - 103 -
Being "Captain" Isn't the Only Requirement to Lead .... - 106 -
The Future Captain: Aaron Judge.................................... - 108 -
Summary of *Player-Led Teams* .... - 111 -

Chapter Six

Community .... - 113 -
    Reinventing the Yankee Stadium Experience .... - 113 -
    9/11 .... - 117 -
    Monument Park and Old Timer's Day .... - 120 -
    HOPE Week .... - 124 -
    Summary of *Community* .... - 127 -
    KEY POINTS: CULTURE–PEOPLE AND COMMUNITY .... - 129 -

PILLAR THREE

PLAYER DEVELOPMENT AND ORGANIZATIONAL STRUCTURE ... - 131 -

Chapter Seven

Scouting and Drafting .... - 133 -
    Using Data and Information, Part I:
    Making Decisions on Talent .... - 133 -
    Summary of *Scouting and Drafting* .... - 138 -

Chapter Eight

Development Isn't Always Linear .... - 139 -
    Talent Development and Distribution .... - 140 -
    Have a Growth Mindset .... - 145 -
    Dealing with External Pressure .... - 147 -
    Summary of *Development Isn't Always Linear* .... - 149 -

Chapter Nine

Moneyball, Sabermetrics, and Analytics .... - 151 -
    Moneyball .... - 153 -
    How Have Moneyball and Analytics Affected the Yankees? .... - 158 -
    Using Data and Information, Part II:
    Gaining a Competitive Edge .... - 163 -
    An Outlook: The Competitive Baseball Landscape .... - 165 -
    Building Depth .... - 166 -
    The Future of Data and Information .... - 167 -
    Summary of *Moneyball, Sabermetrics, and Analytics* .... - 170 -
    KEY POINTS: PLAYER DEVELOPMENT AND
    ORGANIZATIONAL STRUCTURE .... - 171 -

Epilogue

The Future of the Yankees and Creating Your
Culture of Excellence .... - 173 -

Final Points of Emphasis.. - 174 -

Colin's Favorites .... - 176 -

Let the Talent 409 Leadership Academy Help You or Your Team
Discover Your Talent Altitude!...................................... - 177 -

Glossary of Sports Terms.. - 178 -

References .... - 184 -

About the Author.. - 189 -

ACKNOWLEDGEMENTS

This has quite simply been one of the most fun projects I've ever gotten to do. When I started to consider writing a book, I was stuck between wanting to pen this book versus wanting to create a book that focused on just the fundamentals of leadership from my personal experiences and perspectives. While that book may still be on the table in the future, I'm proud of myself for trusting my instinct and putting out there an account based on one of the most influential franchises in the world.

How's that for a humble brag?

In all seriousness, I have to begin by thanking my wife, Christine, who, from the start, encouraged me to write the book I wanted to write, even if it may have been the more difficult choice. Because I didn't have any personal affiliation with the Yankees, it took countless hours of researching and writing for this undertaking to become a reality. Without her love and support, I would have never had the courage or the grit to finish what I started more than three years ago.

I want to thank Phil Gross, a friend and a former work colleague, who wrote a blog post thanking folks that helped him in his own writing journey. This blog was vitally important to the development of my book, because it introduced me to my first editor, Dawn Husted, of Yaupon Berry Press LLC. Dawn helped me strengthen the "bones" of my "shitty first draft" and was instrumental in building the momentum I needed to get to the next stages of the publishing process.

Robin J. Samuels of Shadowcat Editing was there to guide me to the finish line. She brought the clarity to a highly complex story and supported me through some of the most difficult decisions I had to make to get this book out there.

Nina Durfee supported me through the very end and has a wealth of knowledge when it comes to the publishing process.

The team at MIBLART designed the incredible book cover for this story.

Thank you to Gary S. James, jamesgang creative, who designed the layout of this book and made it feel real.

Finally, I want to thank my parents. You couldn't have known it at the time, but when you bought *The 1996 World Series Home Video* for a Christmas gift, you completely transformed me into a fan of baseball and, of course, the Yankees. Without that video, I might not have had any love for the sport or for the Yankees, and I most certainly wouldn't have written this book.

The Bronx Zoo and Birth of a Model Organization

1989

W here we begin this story isn't by accident, as arbitrary as the year may seem. The year 1989 was a momentous time for the purpose of our starting point. No, it's not because it's the year I happened to enter this crazy world. It's not because 1989 meant saying goodbye to the preceding disco decade, or because it began the fall of the Berlin Wall, or because we were still trying to figure out if that sitcom *Seinfeld* was really "a show about nothing."

The year 1989 is important to this story because it marks the turning point of a franchise that had been in turmoil for almost twenty-five years. Starting that year, a series of tragic and dubious decisions would change the fortunes of arguably the most successful and recognizable organization in world-sports history.

The first of these occasions came on December 25, 1989. The site: Port Crane, New York, a small farming area located just north of Binghamton. Billy Martin, the on-again/off-again manager of the New York Yankees, had just finished up another day of carousing with his pal, William Reedy, when Reedy drove his pickup truck into a drainage culvert near Martin's home. Martin, riding in the passenger seat of the truck, was pronounced dead at a hospital shortly after the crash.

The scene that played out on that sad Christmas Day, and later in court, sharply illustrated the nutty atmosphere that engulfed the Yankees during much of George Steinbrenner's first sixteen years as majority owner and general managing partner. Sure, under "the Boss," as Steinbrenner was affectionately known, the franchise briefly returned to relevance during the late 1970s through 1981—even winning two World Series titles in 1977 and 1978—but by all accounts, in 1989 they were a flawed franchise.

A large amount of that dysfunction had been created by Steinbrenner *and* Martin. These men were known for putting the glory of winning above all else and were widely regarded as egotistical. Thus, it was inevitable that they would clash often, and have a difficult time coexisting.

Theirs was a classic love-hate relationship. The Boss fired Martin five times over the course of fourteen years. Each time Martin was fired, the owner wanted his manager back almost as quickly as he had ousted him, resulting in a dizzying cycle of firings and rehirings.

What do they say is the definition of insanity? Doing the same thing over and over and expecting different results? If you had a *Webster*'s *Dictionary* in 1989 and opened it to the page that defined insanity, you could've put a picture of Steinbrenner and Martin shouting at each other. After all, the era *is* regularly referred to by many as the "Bronx Zoo."

Instead of more organizational chaos, 1989 became a defining year for Steinbrenner, for the Yankees, and for the sport of baseball. Martin's death effectively put an end to the charade that was the George and Billy Show, which was rumored to be ramping up for another season at the start of the 1990s. Seriously. Six days before Christmas of 1989, Steinbrenner and Martin were at an annual holiday pageant in Tampa for two thousand underprivileged kids; they had talked about Martin replacing Bucky Dent as manager of the Yankees at the first signs of trouble during the 1990 season.

This may seem like a subjective genesis for a story, and the negative light being shed on Martin and Steinbrenner may seem harsh to the old-school baseball and Yankee fans. But I sincerely believe that the Yankees' ultimate fortunes began to change for the good as an indirect result of Martin's death, which, at the very least, finally allowed for *some* stability to set in at the crucial managerial position.

Subsequent events, with Steinbrenner cast first as the villain and later as the hero, resulted in the Yankees that we all know and love (or hate) today: Between 1990 and 2019, there were fourteen division titles, seven American League pennants, five World Series titles, and countless unforgettable moments.

Why the Yankees?

Thirty years is a long time ago, but it's an excellent period of history to accurately reflect upon. I wrote this book for many reasons, one being my love for the game of baseball. I love the rich history of the game, I love the numbers that are undeniably a part of it, and I love the family connection the sport brings to my life.

As the kids say, *ball is life.*

But the chief reason I'm writing this book is to showcase the Yankees' continuous period of excellence. Throughout the past thirty seasons, the Yankees have experienced a rollercoaster ride of ups and downs, good times and bad, lots of winning, and some painful losses. The Yankees are not a team with one great season or with a handful of competitive seasons before falling out of relevance. A *Culture of Excellence* requires *sustainable* year-over-year results, which allow one to compete at the highest level while dabbling with smaller changes each year that positively impact the organization.

I wanted to write a book that encapsulates how leadership and organizational competence (or lack thereof) lead to people wanting (or not) to be a part of a culture. When doing research for this book, I kept coming back to the fundamental question, *How do culture and leadership impact the performance of a team?* The answer to that question is provided in this book as foundational insight that highlights the on-field *and* off-field elements of success.

What is culture? Culture is interpreted in many different ways, and it's a word that is often too vague or doesn't deliver the appropriate impact. For the purposes of this reading, I define culture as the experiences you have with the people who surround you. It's what you believe. It's how you behave. Thus, one can reason that this book is less about baseball and more about the *people* in the game.

Defining a *Culture of Excellence* requires us to reframe what it means to be great. Too many leaders make decisions based on outcome rather than processes. There are too many teams that focus only on the *Win-Loss* column and neglect everything else that is important.

Adam Grant, the incredible organizational psychologist, once tweeted about culture, "If you define success in terms of winning and losing, you've already lost. The higher you climb, the more your success depends on making others successful."

Winning is great, obviously, and the games are played to determine a champion. But if a team enjoys a season full of wins only to fall short of the championship, that doesn't equate to a total failure. Stringing together a decade or more of sustainability with only one, or even zero, titles to show for it ... that shouldn't be considered a defeat, either.

It should be noted here that great culture doesn't automatically equate to excellence on the field. If you don't have the right mix of talent, then you don't stand a chance to compete at the highest level. There have also been teams with poor cultures who have found themselves on top at season's end. That said, no one ever claimed that a great culture prevented a team from achieving enormous heights. It's only one piece of the puzzle, though an important one.

A great culture can help you attract the right talent and achieve sustainable excellence. Culture can be the foundation upon which you build out everything else. That is what the Yankees can teach us.

Baseball is inherently a game (and business) of failure. The Yankees don't always get it right with their processes, but their vision for success is now more focused on the long term, versus the "win now" mode that was a part of their DNA for so long during the George Steinbrenner era.

The Yankees' current run of excellence has also elevated the game of baseball. Their success has forced other teams to find innovative ways to be competitive, such as using analytics to find market inefficiencies, and that has altered the landscape to be arguably more balanced today than ever before in the sport's history.

Like the Golden State Warriors in the National Basketball Association (NBA), Alabama Crimson Tide in college football, and Ronda Rousey for the Ultimate Fighting Championship (UFC), the Yankees have had an impact on baseball that will affect the way it's played and how teams operate, long after this book is written.

As such, the biggest challenge the Yankees face is to continuously improve. It's actually not as easy a task as the franchise has made it look. Their consistency shines even brighter, given that they could easily have fallen into complacency at any time.

I'm not here to tell you everything the Yankees do is the only way to do business correctly. There are many ways the Yankees—and baseball as a whole—could be doing better, like hiring more women and people of color into positions of influence and leadership. But that is a conversation for another day. This account centers solely on how the Yankees became the modern powerhouse and cultural model they are, and what they are doing to keep their competitive edge.

What Is There to Be Discovered?

Let me be the first to say that you *will* uncover incredible stories in this book. But you may be thinking, "Who is this guy, and why should I listen to him?" Here's why: I began my career in Recruiting and Human Resources, where I built a skill set focused on training others in leadership and group dynamics. Pairing this experience with knowledge from my time as a college athlete, I started my own consulting firm, the Talent 409 Leadership Academy. My days are now dedicated to helping individuals grow into more effective leaders and developing teams that have a thriving, compelling culture.

Sports and culture are what I do.

Plus, I love the Yankees!

That's why *I'm* the one that gets to write this book.

In this book, we will discuss three main pillars:

1. *Leadership*
2. *Culture–People and Community*
3. *Player Development and Organizational Structure*

Building on that backbone, we will see how this acts as a foundation to the many additional characteristics that define a *Culture of Excellence*.

Reader Tip: There is also a *Glossary of Sports Terms* located in the back of the book for anyone who isn't familiar with the lingo.

My sincere hope is that you are able to take the Yankees' model of sustainability, their lessons in leadership and organizational development, and incorporate them into your team or business immediately, while also forming a new appreciation for America's Favorite Pastime.

So, without further ado, let's play ball!

PILLAR ONE

LEADERSHIP

Leadership *(noun)* - the power or ability to lead other people

"I hold on to competent people so that they can make decisions that don't involve me."

- Hal Steinbrenner

Chapter One

The Boss

T he scope of a leader's responsibility (and influence) in modern sports has changed dramatically over time, and never before has there been more at stake for the position. Given the enormous revenue taken in and investments handed out, it's more important now than at any point in history to have strong organizational leadership—from top to bottom. The gamble is too high, and the financial impact is too great, to have leaders that produce dumpster-fire results. No longer can leaders carouse and repeatedly prove themselves incompetent without facing public ridicule or putting their job in serious jeopardy.

Leadership sits at the core of explaining the factors that influence good or bad business decisions. Thus, this book's examination of influential figures within the New York Yankees' franchise. Understanding the folks at the top of command—ownership, front-office executives, managers, and coaches—helps us better discern the entire organizational structure and philosophy.

I believe that there is no better person to start with than a man simply known as "the Boss."

Who Is the Boss?

George Michael Steinbrenner III was born on July 4, 1930, in Rocky River, Ohio. From birth, it seemed that Steinbrenner's father, Henry, instilled in his son a perfectionism and will-to-win-competitiveness that came to define his management style and tenure with the Yankees.

Steinbrenner was a football guy, growing up watching the Big Ten Conference in college football and also playing the sport. During his youth, victory came through team play, self-confidence, and enthusiasm that amounted to the highest level of dedication; but most importantly, American football players in the mid-twentieth century were known for their tireless and committed work ethic. That persona came to describe the man who later became known as the Boss.

By 1967, before his baseball career, Steinbrenner became the majority owner of his father's shipbuilding business, the American Ship Building Company, where he got his first taste of the entrepreneurial world. The Boss flexed his businessman's muscles and proved himself to be adept at leading the company; he dramatically increased revenue from $46.9 million in his first year to $73.7 million by 1972. But, while the family business was good to him, Steinbrenner was desperate for a career "sexier" than that of shipbuilding.

In 1971, he had a shot to shoot: the Cleveland Indians were for sale, and Steinbrenner put together an investment group to strike a deal for his hometown Major League Baseball (MLB) team. On December 6, Steinbrenner and his group agreed to buy the Indians for $8.6 million. Steinbrenner was joyful at the thought of entering into the sports industry, telling people, "This is my dream. I can do this. I have the people with the money."

One can only assume the rage that must have ensued when Steinbrenner learned the deal had been killed at the last minute by the Indians' then-majority owner, Vernon Stouffer. Stouffer thought he could get $10 million from someone else for the franchise (which he eventually did), and Steinbrenner thought his chance to make an impact in sports was over. Little did he know that a more promising opportunity would present itself just about a year later.

A Brief History Lesson About the Yankees

The New York Yankees have one of the richest histories in sports. Legends such as Babe Ruth, Reggie Jackson, and Mariano Rivera have donned the famous Yankee pinstripes. When the Yankees purchased Ruth from the Boston Red Sox in 1920, the franchise catapulted into an unprecedented run, which saw them win twenty-nine American League (AL) pennants and twenty World Series in a forty-five-year period. Never before or since has there been such an impressive streak of dominance, not just in baseball, but in all of sports.

Nevertheless, it's true that anything good must come to an end. The conclusion of the Yankees' superiority led them into a dark period that few would have ever predicted. In 1964, CBS, the broadcast television and radio network, bought 80 percent of the Yankees from partners Dan Topping and Del Webb, and two years later would purchase the remaining 20 percent stake from the former majority owners. But from the start, it was clear that the marriage between the powerhouse station and baseball's most mighty franchise would not be a happy one.

The fall of the "old-time" Yankees can be at least partially attributed to poor business practices prior to CBS's entering the equation. In 1962, Topping and Webb began cutting investments in younger players, which left the CBS ownership with an aging roster of superstars and few capable replacements. The club was also very resistant to signing African American ballplayers, and throughout the 1940s and 1950s they repeatedly missed out on stars they had legitimate opportunities to sign, such as future Hall of Famers Hank Aaron and Willie Mays.

By the end of 1971, the CBS-led Yankees had rung up a loss of $11 million.[1] The loss was driven by declining game attendance, television revenues that fell 80 percent from their peak, and worst of all, they had become second-class citizens in their own city, thanks to the rise of the start-up Mets.

---

[1] CBS purchased the Yankees for $11.2 million.

The Yankees made the playoffs a total of zero times under CBS's guidance and posted losing records four times, finishing tenth out of ten teams in 1966. The Mets, meanwhile, captured their first World Series title in 1969, and they had promising young talent to power them for subsequent title runs.

The future of the Yankees was in serious doubt, but the question remained: *Could they return to prominence under more capable leadership?*

During negotiations for the Indians in 1971, George Steinbrenner developed an alliance with the Indians' Vice President of Operations, Gabe Paul. Paul, a baseball junkie, had strong relationships with almost all the owners and top officials in baseball. After the failed Indians sale, Steinbrenner instructed Paul to let him know if another franchise went on the market. In the summer of 1972, Paul caught wind that CBS was putting the Yankees up for sale, and he informed Steinbrenner, who immediately put together a group to purchase the franchise, including many of the same people from the unsuccessful Cleveland transaction.

CBS had failed mightily in its attempt to lead the Yankees, and Steinbrenner saw his second attempt at baseball glory as only a formality. Negotiations moved fast between CBS and the Steinbrenner-led group. The purchase was completed on December 29, 1972, for $8.7 million, and the breakdown gave Steinbrenner the largest individual interest at 11 percent, totaling $168,000.

George Steinbrenner had officially entered the world of baseball.

Steinbrenner's Vision for Excellence (1973–1990)

When George Steinbrenner bought the Yankees, he had a vision of returning the franchise to prominence. It's a process that all leaders undergo as they lay the foundation for a bigger and better future.[2]

One of the first projects Steinbrenner supervised was the renovation of the original Yankee Stadium. Opened in 1923, it was the first facility in North America with three tiers, and it held historical significance, as it symbolized the glory days of the Yankees. By the time Steinbrenner took control of the organization, the stadium had seen better days, both structurally and from the Yankees' team. The change was needed, and Steinbrenner made sure the plan, which was designed before he officially took over, was completed to his expectations.

The results of the restoration were mind-blowing for the time. The outside of the stadium remained mostly the same, but on the inside 118 columns reinforcing each tier of the grandstand were removed. These columns had long restricted visibility for paying patrons, and their removal allowed for more of a full-field view.[3]

The stadium's roof and metal frieze (the facade) were replaced by a new upper shell, and brighter lights were added above. The playing field was lowered by seven feet, and new drainage was installed. Escalators and ramps were added in three sections to make the upper deck more accessible. A new middle tier was built, featuring a larger press box and sixteen luxury boxes. The middle section of the center field bleachers was converted to "the black seats," which is a safety feature ensuring the white baseball wouldn't disappear from the view of the hitter. A wall was built behind the bleachers, and on it was the first instant replay display in baseball.

---

[2] Take, for example, basketball's Dallas Mavericks. When Mark Cuban purchased the Mavericks, the *Shark Tank* investor insisted on a new team plane, new uniforms, improved locker rooms, and an upgraded arena. Cuban didn't wait to see results before making a significant bet on his franchise's future. He decided that if the culture in Dallas was going to change to a winning one, it was starting from day one, and it began with him.

[3] *Author's note:* My grandpa and dad actually went to Yankee games during the 1960s and had tickets behind "column seats." Luckily, there usually wasn't a sell-out crowd and they were able to easily move to a less obstructed view of the field and game.

In short, Steinbrenner had the intuition to realize that the *fan experience* in the ballpark had to improve, in addition to his on-field team, if he wanted to see an increase in ticket sales.

The Boss was also a pioneer for the free-agency movement in baseball, which is an open market of ballplayers, if you will. In the early 1970s, many baseball owners saw free agency as a tactic that would kill the game, but Steinbrenner's vision was different. He saw it as a way to rebuild the Yankees even faster *and* had a willingness to open up his checkbook to make it happen.

The Boss's first major catch in free agency came on New Year's Eve of 1974, when he inked Jim "Catfish" Hunter to a five-year, $3.25 million deal. Then on November 29, 1976—fresh off the team's first World Series appearance since 1964—Steinbrenner signed Reggie Jackson to a five-year, $3.5 million contract which, at the time, made the Yankees' new right fielder the highest-paid player in the game. One year later, on November 23, 1977, Rich "Goose" Gossage signed a six-year, $3.6 million deal to complete a formidable bullpen for a club that had just won its first World Series since 1962.

During those times, more often than not, when the Boss needed to fill weak spots, he could plug those holes with players via free agency. Initially, it was a formula that worked; Steinbrenner quickly rebuilt the Yankees' franchise, and by 1976 they were once again a perennial playoff contender. The Yankees were swept four games to none in that year's World Series by the Big Red Machine (Cincinnati Reds) but returned to the World Series in each of the next two seasons, beating the Los Angeles Dodgers in six games each time.

Unfortunately, the euphoria of the new Yankees dynasty would erode quickly. In 1979, the Yankees slid to fourth in the standings. They returned to the playoffs in 1980 but were swept by the Kansas City Royals, three games to none, in the American League Championship Series (ALCS). In the strike-shortened 1981 season, they made it back to the World Series but fell to the Dodgers in six games. Few people, inside or outside of baseball, would have predicted that it would be fourteen seasons before the Yankees would return to postseason play.

Steinbrenner's Leadership Profile

There used to be a wooden nameplate at Yankee Stadium atop George Steinbrenner's desk, engraved with the motto, "LEAD, FOLLOW, OR GET THE HELL OUT OF THE WAY." This was a reference to United States Army General George Patton, a person Steinbrenner admired greatly, so it's no surprise that Steinbrenner's leadership style closely resembled that of the former American military leader.

Both Steinbrenner and Patton have at times been described as misinterpreted. What's not misunderstood is that Steinbrenner was a "hard-nosed businessman," "impulsive and demanding," and "manic, fiercely competitive, and frequently guilty of outrageous behavior." In public, he could be a tyrant and a bully. "The mad shipbuilder," as he was also known, was obsessive, unforgiving, and hands-on during his reign as Yankees owner.

Former Yankees shortstop Tony Kubek, at the time a broadcaster, complained in a 1978 op-ed to the *Fort Lauderdale News* that Steinbrenner "manipulates people and makes players fear for their jobs."

Obviously, Steinbrenner's behavior is not quite what one thinks of when they envision a *leader*—at least not an effective one. Steinbrenner's first "term" (1973–1990) as commander-in-chief would accurately reflect his conduct. The Yankees, on and off the field, were in a constant state of chaos. Steinbrenner shuffled general managers fourteen times in his first seventeen seasons, in addition to seventeen on-field managerial changes.

It seemed continuity was impossible to achieve under the Boss's watch.

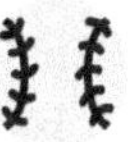

Regardless of the instability, George Steinbrenner had more energy than anyone in the Yankees' organization, and he set the pace for the entire franchise. Tom Verducci, of *Sports Illustrated*, wrote in his collaborative book with (former Yankees' manager) Joe Torre, *The Yankee Years*, that, "Unlike most of the other owners, who busied themselves with their business world interests and found pockets of time to check on their baseball team, Steinbrenner went to bed at night and woke up in the morning with the same thought: *We have to win*. He was ruthless in his goal."

Steinbrenner always had a willingness to pour money back into the Yankees; he was *never* concerned—and maybe wrongfully so—about keeping a profit. The Boss saw other franchises determined to lock down on budgets to increase profits or reduce loss. What's the biggest problem with this philosophy? It made these franchises far less competitive. Taking money from fans and making the prosperous richer would never be the primary motive as long as Steinbrenner was running the Yankees.

Steinbrenner was committed to the Yankees, and for all his shortcomings, he was as competent as any owner in baseball history. How rare is the "competent" attribute? Liz Ryan, a former senior vice president of Human Resources and best-selling author of *Reinvention Roadmap: Break the Rules to Get the Job You Want and Career You Deserve*, says there are five signs of an incompetent leader. Of the five signs, Steinbrenner particularly defied three of them:

1.   *They have no vision.*
2.   *They can't get off the dime (which means to take action).*
3.   *They can't react to changing circumstances.*

With regard to those three signs, Steinbrenner's competency shines through: his vision when he bought the Yankees was to restore the franchise to prominence, which he did when they won the World Series in 1977 and 1978. Taking action was never a problem for Steinbrenner, and as owner, he was often too decisive. But he never sat back and waited for opportunities to create themselves. Finally, the Boss reacted positively to the changing baseball landscape in the mid-1970s, as he was a free-agency pioneer and struck a $486 million television deal with MSG in 1988—unheard-of sums at the time.

Steinbrenner was not perfect, and though he went through extreme highs and lows for his legacy to be remembered as it is today, the Boss was not one to skimp on his responsibilities as a leader.

Leading with Empathy

Beneath Steinbrenner's Winter Warlock layers of icy ruthlessness lay a softer side that could melt even the Grinchiest soul. "That's the way George was," said Joe Torre, the manager of the Yankees from 1996 to 2007. "When you were suffering, he'd come help you. Otherwise, he'd be this tyrant who would second-guess a lot of stuff that you did or didn't do."

Joe Girardi, a player and manager under Steinbrenner, added, "George was responsible for the best years of my life, professionally. Did we get along all the time? No. But it never lasted very long. I always felt we had a special relationship. George was so devoted to this city and these fans."

His devotion to the city of New York and the Yankee fans *was* a major contributor to the Boss's manic demeanor, but that was hardly the only factor. Steinbrenner *hated* to lose, and people close to him confessed that he distrusted success.

The Boss once instructed that adversity is the greatest teacher, while success is the shortest lesson. He would convince himself that success would make his employees soft, so when the Yankees won, he would push even harder.

The responsibility of owning the Yankees and the pressure to win in New York were reasons why Steinbrenner, at times, acted as maddeningly as he did. But when it mattered, the Boss could be warm, welcoming, and *helpful*.

⚾

It is quite possible that George Steinbrenner's best moment as the leader and owner of the Yankees came during what was arguably the most difficult situation for the franchise.

Thurman Munson played parts of eleven seasons with the Yankees, primarily as their everyday catcher. Munson was named Rookie of the Year in 1970, appeared in seven All-Star Games, and was the 1976 Most Valuable Player (MVP).

Munson was an instrumental part of the Steinbrenner-led rebuild in the early to mid-1970s because of his production on the field as well as his leadership on *and* off of it. He was so highly regarded by the Boss and the Yankees that he was named captain in 1976—the first player to receive the honor since former first baseman Lou Gehrig retired in 1939.

Munson was a tough-natured grouch who was the ideal person to navigate the Yankees through the Bronx Zoo and the constant disarray created by Steinbrenner and manager Billy Martin. For everything Steinbrenner and Martin were, Munson was almost the complete opposite.

As captain, Munson guided the Yankees to back-to-back championships in 1977 and 1978, fittingly catching the final out of the '78 World Series. But by 1979, he was beginning to seriously consider his long-term future in New York and in baseball. Munson was experiencing physical pains due to the demands of being an everyday catcher, and he was also a committed family man. It gnawed at him to be away from his wife, Diana, and his three kids for long stretches during the brutal baseball seasons.

Munson, ever resourceful, wound up obtaining his pilot's license, and flew home so often between games, leaving after one and returning in time for the next, that he didn't even have a permanent New York residence for the season. Munson loved to fly so he could spend more time with his family, but he also loved the solitude of being alone in the air and getting away from the grind of the baseball season.

Flying into his hometown of Canton, Ohio, on August 1, 1979, Munson arrived safely, but he felt there was something wrong with his new higher-powered jet airplane. During a Yankees off-day on August 2, he decided to run a series of "touch-and-go" tests to resolve the plane's issues before heading back to New York. On one of the final tests, Munson was not able to successfully land the plane, and he crashed it just one thousand feet away from the runway. Upon the crash landing, the plane lost its wings and burst into flames, resulting in injuries to two occupants—including the person who had taught

Munson how to fly—and the death of a third occupant, who was later confirmed by a Summit County sheriff to be Munson.

Thurman Munson was just thirty-two years old.

The Yankees were rocked by the shocking news of Munson's death. His manager at the time, Billy Martin, said of the catcher, "For those who never knew him and didn't like him, I feel sorry for them. He was a great man, for his family, friends and all the people who knew and loved him, my deepest sympathy. We not only lost a great competitor, but a leader and a husband and devoted family man. He was a close friend, I loved him."

The Yankees had a game to play the night after Munson's unexpected death. Appropriately enough, it was a dark, cold, and rainy night in the Bronx, which began with a pregame ceremony to honor their fallen captain. The team lost that game 1–0, but the surreal reality of the situation was that there were more games to be played without Munson and a funeral still to be had on his behalf.

Munson's burial took place on August 6, and eulogies were given by many Yankee teammates, including Bobby Murcer, the last Yankees player to see Munson before he took off to Canton. The Yankees also had a scheduled game that day, and they returned to New York that night in time to play the Baltimore Orioles.

The Orioles jumped out to a 4–0 lead, and in a game in which it would have been easily excusable for them to quit, the Yankees summoned the courage to stop the bleeding at four, and began to mount a comeback.

Murcer hit a three-run homer in the bottom of the seventh inning to cut the Orioles' lead to 4–3. Then, in the bottom of the ninth, with the Yankees still down 4–3, Murcer again came up and laced a ball down the left-field line that scored two. That gave the Yankees one of their most remarkable regular-season wins in franchise history. On the day they buried their captain, the Yankees showed ultimate strength and fortitude by banding together and pulling through in a true moment of adversity.

If that were the only story of how the Yankees reacted to the end of Thurman Munson's life, then it would be good enough for most people. But there is another story from within that took shape because of the actions of George Steinbrenner. When the Boss passed away in 2010, Diana Munson took to the *Daily News* to give her recollection of the immediate aftermath of the death of her husband.

"And then, when Thurman passed away," Diana began. "I saw an entirely different side of George. I saw a man who was soft and gentle and unbelievably kind.

"Here I was a thirty-year-old widow with three young children. It was very overwhelming. George understood that, and really, he could not have done enough for us as a family."

For twenty-nine years, until the Yankees' final game in the old Yankee Stadium, Munson's locker was preserved in the clubhouse as a reminder of their fallen captain. It was a great tribute paid to a man who meant so much to the team. Of the gesture, Diana would say, "George showed our family so much kindness for so many years, but the fact that he kept Thurman's locker that way as a living memorial touched me more than anything else he could've done."

Steinbrenner was also instrumental in providing the necessary stability (how ironic) while arrangements were being made for Munson's funeral and the Yankee Stadium memorial. The Boss spearheaded all those efforts and let everyone else, from Munson's family to the Yankees, grieve and come to grips with the grim position they were all in.

Steinbrenner was at his best as a leader in a time of true crisis, and it's a moment in time that anyone associated with the Yankees, especially the Munson family, will never forget.

"He let me know the day of Thurman's passing that I wouldn't be alone in it," Diana Munson said of Steinbrenner. "Being a young woman, a mother of three young children, I knew there was someone there for me.

"I didn't test that promise, but just knowing someone was there in the background gave me reassurance. It gave me strength."

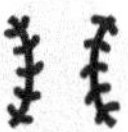

Steinbrenner found ways to extend himself with other people throughout the years. After Yankees manager Bob Lemon was fired in 1982, he was given a lifetime scouting contract by the Boss for $50,000 per year. Steinbrenner could be "heartless and magnanimous in almost the same gesture," wrote his biographer, Bill Madden.

Also in 1982, after attending the funeral of a police officer killed in the line of duty, Steinbrenner started the Silver Shield Foundation. The Boss, after seeing the saddened young children of the slain cop, was concerned about their future educational costs. The Foundation was created to set aside an education fund for each surviving child to assist with tuition payments for prep school, college and university undergraduate and graduate school, vocational and technical school, and tutoring services.

From inception until 2000, Silver Shield paid for the college educations of more than two hundred sons and daughters of New York City police and fire officials, New York Port Authority officers, and New York, New Jersey, and Connecticut state troopers killed in the line of duty. After the tragedy of 9/11, Silver Shield paid for an additional seven hundred more educations. By 2010, the foundation's endowment was nearly $4 million.

The End of Steinbrenner's "First Term" as Owner

George Steinbrenner was the most powerful person in the Yankees' organization during his time as an owner. In 1989, while he may have been *powerful*, he wasn't too *popular*.

In August of that year, Steinbrenner fired then-manager Dallas Green and replaced him with 1978 playoff hero Bucky Dent. This marked *the seventeenth time in seventeen seasons* that the owner of the Yankees canned the person leading the players on the field. This was a period when being Steinbrenner's manager could be referred to as "a temporary position."

The night Green was fired, the fans at Yankee Stadium publicly displayed their displeasure with the Boss by chanting in unison, "George must go! George must go!" The Yankees finished the 1989 season in fifth place, and at 74–87 it was the team's worst record since 1967, five years before Steinbrenner purchased the Yankees from CBS.

Meanwhile, Steinbrenner's private life was also in upheaval. American Ship Building Company, the business he purchased from his father in 1963, had seen its fortunes decline sharply as the landscape around the country changed. The company was hemorrhaging money. His team stunk, his shipbuilding business was sinking, and there was another storm brewing, caused primarily by the Boss's own indiscretion.

In 1989, it was no secret that George Steinbrenner and Dave Winfield, the Yankees' handsomely paid right fielder, did not like each other. But this relationship wasn't a love-hate with Billy Martin, and it wasn't a feud with Reggie Jackson; this cratering connection was entirely different from any other the Boss ever had.

On December 15, 1980, Winfield signed with the Yankees for a then record-setting ten years and $23 million. At the time, Steinbrenner boasted joyfully about his latest prized acquisition in free agency. But by the end of the 1980s, the once-rosy relationship between Winfield and Steinbrenner had deteriorated significantly, so much that the Boss paid off known gambler Howie Spira for information regarding The Winfield Foundation, because he felt that Winfield wasn't correctly allocating the money coming in to the charity. Steinbrenner was looking "to unearth embarrassing information about Winfield."

Nobody outside of Steinbrenner's circle had any idea of the owner's shady business tactic until March 18, 1990, when the *Daily News* released an exclusive front-page report written by Richard Pienciak. Pienciak had gotten ahold of tapes that Spira had recorded during his conversations with Steinbrenner, and Pienciak had also obtained photocopies of two payment checks Steinbrenner allegedly wrote to Spira.

On March 23, Spira was indicted for extortion, and MLB Commissioner Fay Vincent announced to the public he was looking into the payments made by Steinbrenner. By mid-spring 1990, Vincent was conducting a full-scale investigation of the Boss's involvement with Spira, and in early May, Steinbrenner's deposition was taken.

Less than a month after his sixtieth birthday, on July 30, 1990, Steinbrenner went to Commissioner Vincent's office and learned he would be suspended—the second time in his tenure as the Yankees' owner—for two years, followed by a three-year probation period, for his involvement with Spira. (Steinbrenner had also been suspended in 1974 after he was indicted on fourteen counts of illegal campaign donations made to United States President Richard Nixon's reelection campaign.)

At the time of the second suspension, Steinbrenner was also the vice president of the United States Olympic Committee and did not want to lose the position as a result of his baseball suspension. As such, Vincent gave Steinbrenner another option, one that would allow him to focus solely on his Olympic efforts: voluntarily resign as Yankees' managing general partner, remove himself from the day-to-day operations of the club, and go on baseball's permanently ineligible list.

To everyone's astonishment, Steinbrenner agreed to the terms. Shortly after the news became public, he told the press, "I want out of baseball" and "I'm sick and tired of it." That night, the crowd at Yankee Stadium reacted to the report of Steinbrenner's ban by chanting happily, "No more George! No more George! No more George!"

The Boss's formal resignation came to Commissioner Vincent's office in a two-paragraph note at 9:00 a.m. on August 21, 1990, to be effective at 12:01 a.m. the next morning.

The Yankees' record at the time of Steinbrenner's resignation stood at 50–70. It was an unfavorable transformation: Steinbrenner had gone from rescuing and restoring the Yankees in the late 1970s to being vilified and completely out of baseball eighteen years later.

The Start of Steinbrenner's "Second Term" as Owner (1993–2010)

On July 23, 1992, it was announced that the Boss "would be allowed to resume active control of the Yankees on March 1, 1993." Behind the scenes, the other owners and powerful people in baseball had done their own digging into Steinbrenner's permanent ban and had come to the conclusion that Fay Vincent had abused his powers as commissioner of the sport. Incredibly enough, *they* wanted Steinbrenner back in the fold because they found Vincent's behavior even more unacceptable.

The Boss was back. The only question that lingered over the sport and the Yankees was not *if*, but *when*, his reign would bring chaos like before.

Summary of *The Boss*

It's difficult to predict how the course of history may have been changed had George Steinbrenner not been suspended in 1990. Life is funny like that. Oftentimes a person must undergo a true moment of adversity to see the harm they may be causing. Until that *Oh shit!* moment, people live their life without knowing the adjustments they need to make.

In the case of Steinbrenner, he *did* change, and as a result, the Yankees' good fortunes would continue to mount forward. The Boss's teams wound up winning a total of seven World Series championships and eleven American League pennants during his full tenure as owner of the Yankees. The second "term" with Steinbrenner will be told in more detail throughout the remaining pages, but it's important to note here that the Boss's significant influence on the Yankees' organization—and the game of baseball—will endure into the future as it has for the immortal Babe Ruth.

Steinbrenner was brash, curt, and at times, a person with serious judgment flaws. But he was also a pioneer, and he had a willingness and a desire to invest in what he believed in to make his franchise first class through and through.

The Yankees have a lot of money, and they are proud of it; it's a defining Steinbrenner legacy. Beyond the money that Steinbrenner spent, the Boss was able to create a culture that has an *unrivaled* passion for winning. In return, the Yankees feel the ultimate responsibility to field a contender year after year.

The Boss has been dead for ten years, but that passion for winning is as strong as ever. That's how powerful George Steinbrenner was. One wonders, had he come from a different time and background, would he have allowed his gentler side to be seen more often? But this is who Steinbrenner was; and he will always, unmistakably, be remembered as a Yankee and for his sincere desire to win above all else.

Chapter Two

The Manager's Seat

In the basic organizational structure, leadership is important at every level. C-suite-level bosses often get the most attention, but middle managers' scope of responsibility is arguably of greater importance, even if the people in those positions may not have the full influence of a high-level executive.

This perception is never more apparent than in the world of sports, where managers and head coaches often get too much credit or too much blame. Coaches are out on the field and in the public eye, while owners and front-office executives can hide in their big, private offices and avoid answering media questions. This is one of the biggest differentiators between middle management in sports and that in corporate business, which is much more private and behind the scenes.

With the increased visibility in sports comes a surge of responsibility and pressure. That becomes magnified in a city like New York. New York City is the largest media market in *North America*, home to many of the biggest media outlets and their job is pretty straightforward: hunt for content to provide to the public during the modern 24-hours-a-day, 365-days-a-year news cycle.

Early in the George Steinbrenner era, traditional newspapers and tabloids dominated the publication scene. While the market wasn't as instantaneously connected as in modern times, New York City's media has always been considered more difficult to navigate and can even be a harsh burden of responsibility for a certain type of individual.

Billy Martin was *not* that type of person. As the manager during the 1970s and 1980s, he was often too eager to provide reporters with quotes that filled their notebooks with juicy stories. If it wasn't a quote, it was an on-field scene. Sometimes it was both.

One of the more infamous moments of the Bronx Zoo came on June 18, 1977, a day the Yankees played the Boston Red Sox on national television. In the bottom of the sixth inning, and with the Yankees trailing 7–3, Boston's Jim Rice came to bat. Rice hit a soft fly ball that dropped and rolled to Yankees right fielder, Reggie Jackson. The hit turned into a "hustle double"[4] for Rice, and put runners on second and third with one out.

Martin was promptly enraged; he thought Jackson had made a lackadaisical attempt during the play, and in the Yankees' dugout, Martin told backup outfielder Paul Blair to run out and immediately replace Jackson. As shown in video replay, Jackson was clearly surprised by Blair's incoming presence in right field. When Jackson returned to the dugout, he and Martin came face-to-face and had to be separated two different times by Yankees coaches before Jackson eventually left the dugout for the visitors' clubhouse in a fit of rage.[5]

It was an embarrassing scene in Boston that day for the Yankees, fueled by Martin's temper and his disdain for Steinbrenner's cherished off-season acquisition of Jackson. Making matters worse, after the game, Martin told reporters, "If you don't hustle, I don't accept it. If a player shows up the club, I show up the player."

Martin, as was often his script, couldn't let the moment die in the dugout. His quote displays immaturity. He had to get the last shots in on Jackson and feed ammunition to the people who loved him the most: the New York media.

---

[4] A "hustle double" is when a hitter runs hard out of the batter's box and turns a single into a double.
[5] Elston Howard, Yogi Berra, and Dick Howser.

Had this brouhaha happened today, it's fair to wonder if Martin would have survived the social-media barrage that would inevitably have occurred. Martin did remain manager for the rest of the 1977 season and led the Yankees to their twenty-first World Series title.

Martin's publicly embarrassing incidents continued. In 1978, he was off-handedly chatting with media cronies when he called Reggie Jackson a born liar and George Steinbrenner a convicted felon, also saying the owner and right fielder "deserved each other." The quote made it to the newspaper and led to Martin's resigning in disgrace midway through the season.

In addition to the near-fight in the dugout with Jackson in 1977, Martin was later involved in a hotel bar brawl with Yankees pitcher Eddie Lee Whitson in 1985, during Martin's fourth stint as manager. Whitson was angry with Martin for the way the manager made use of the pitcher during the season. The two crossed paths at the hotel bar one night in Baltimore, began arguing, and the argument turned into a fistfight. The incident left Martin in a cast for his broken arm, and it was another item in a laundry list of embarrassing moments for the franchise under his guidance.[6]

The ineptitude that Martin displayed as manager of the Yankees is almost as comical as it is disturbing. Fortunately, today's leaders, visible or not, are held to a higher standard of accountability than they were during Billy Martin's time as manager of the Yankees.

Building a New Foundation: Life Without the Boss

The 1990 Yankees, in the midst of the Steinbrenner suspension, finished the season with a whimper. Their 67–95 record, the poorest showing for the franchise since 1912, was the *worst* of all American League teams.[7] Only the Atlanta Braves could claim to be more inferior in all of baseball that season, with a record of 65–97.

---

[6] Martin was manager of the Yankees for five separate stints between 1975 and his death in 1989.

[7] And they also parted ways with the estranged Dave Winfield, trading him to the California Angels in mid-May.

Gene Michael—a former Yankees player, coach, and manager—was unceremoniously left in charge of the on-field product during Steinbrenner's absence. The terrible record the Yankees produced in 1990 was worrisome for Michael, but not as much as what had transpired in the Yankees' clubhouse. Michael discovered that years of greedy, egotistic, and self-centered players had filed in one after another and created an atmosphere so toxic that it rivaled that of the White House under Donald Trump.

Former Yankees outfielder Luis Polonia reflected on that time period, saying, "This wasn't even a team then. It was a bunch of guys worried about numbers and trying to get their money. Guys rooted for others to screw up so they'd get a chance to play."

That quote by Polonia puts into perspective the circumstances that Michael dealt with during that time while reconstructing the Yankees. It was a dire situation, and the environment desperately needed to change if there were to be any chance of returning the franchise to prominence.

Fortunately, Michael had a plan: he would start by ridding the Yankees of detrimentally selfish and bad teammates. He was also ready to make a change of manager, and after Stump Merrill led the club to an uninspiring 71–91 record in 1991, Michael saw the moment for a new voice.

The manager's seat was given to a man named Buck Showalter, who was hired for the 1992 season and immediately gave the Yankees a much-needed fresh perspective. As a manager, Merrill was loose around his players, but also unorganized. Showalter was the complete opposite; organized almost to a fault and hungry to prove he could manage in the big leagues, even though he never made it past minor league AAA ball as a player.

As a coach and manager, Showalter came from the lower levels of the Yankees' organization. He managed multiple minor-league squads before being promoted to the coaching staff of the big-league ball club in 1990, and he had an appreciation for the Yankees' history that rooted deep in his philosophy as a leader.

While manager of the Yankees, Showalter went on to win 313 games in four seasons. He got to the postseason in 1995, but he'd never get further than the first round of the playoffs.

During the 1995 American League Division Series (ALDS), Showalter inexplicably lost faith in his closing pitcher, John Wetteland, after Wetteland surrendered a long home run to Ken Griffey Jr. in Game 2 of the series, a game the Yankees won 7–5 in fifteen innings. Wetteland successfully finished thirty-one games for the Yankees during the regular season, pitching in mostly high-pressure, late-game situations. But after Wetteland struggled once again in Game 4, Showalter determined he would not use one of his most important pitchers in a classic "win-or-go-home" Game 5.

During Game 5, the Yankees' starting pitcher David Cone would throw 147 pitches, and fellow starter Jack McDowell made the first relief appearance of his career. With Wetteland sitting in the bullpen in the eleventh inning of an elimination game, McDowell surrendered the hit that scored the tying and game-winning runs for the Mariners, winning the series and sending the Yankees home for the long winter.

The Yankees' 1995 season had ended bitterly, and seemingly just as quickly as it started, the Buck Showalter era would be over too.

The Birth of the Joe Torre Era

One of the biggest faults of the corporate world is when a company refuses to hire from the outside, especially for its leadership positions. How can a business expect to get fresh and innovative ideas if they solely rely on hiring from within? The worst of it is that people from within may not be capable of leading, now or in the future.

In an effort to retain its current employees and to sell their ability to grow these individuals, companies repeatedly make the egregious decision to promote someone who isn't ready for a leadership role. Executives let a mantra that shouldn't exist in the first place—*We only hire from within for our management and supervisory positions, so you have a great opportunity to grow with us—*

get in the way of making an astute hire. Let the following be read loud and clear for all to hear:

> *When it comes to hiring someone to be a leader of people, no bigger mistake can be made than to hire someone who is not capable of leading people. If there isn't a person within an organization qualified to lead, then it's time to go outside and hunt for that individual. Do not promote the internal candidate just so they won't get their feelings hurt.*

A new type of leadership profile began to emerge in the precious manager position for the Yankees during the 1990s, one that would become less and less Steinbrenner-esque as the years passed. Gene Michael was making sure of that.

Trust, stability, and relationship-building were at the top of the list for a new era of Yankees managers. Gone would be the days of hothead tempers, backstabbing in private and public, and a complete disregard for organizational stability.

By the end of the 1995 season, and with Steinbrenner back in the fold, the Yankees had a real opportunity to end their championship drought by making a *smart* baseball hire into their manager's seat. Buck Showalter was not retained after the Yankees' crushing five-game ALDS loss to the Seattle Mariners. Inside the clubhouse, players were relieved to know that Showalter wouldn't be returning for a fifth season. They were fed up with his micromanaging, and too many players on the team had lost confidence in his ability to lead.

While the Mariners' dramatic series comeback win saved baseball in the city of Seattle, it also meant the Boss—back in the postseason for the first time since 1981—was hungrier than ever to go deeper in the playoffs. After Showalter declined a two-year offer by the Yankees, the manager's seat was once again open.

Michael thought that with a little more tweaking, the team was ready to "win now," and because of that, he wanted to bring in an experienced manager from outside the organization—Michael didn't feel that there was an internal option ready to lead the major league club. The manager who met Michael's requirements ended up being Joseph Paul Torre, a man who had zero ties to the Yankees and had never played, coached, or managed in the American League.

Torre was a complete outsider. As manager, he had been fired three times by three different teams, was fifty-five years old, and had zero postseason victories on his résumé, which included a regular-season losing record.[8] Torre also had the unfortunate distinction of being the guy with the most games ever played and managed *without* a World Series appearance.

As a player, Torre won a Most Valuable Player award in 1971, went to the All-Star Game nine times as a catcher, and had more than 2,300 career hits. As a manager, he was far less appealing, especially for a franchise—not to mention a fan base—that wanted more than ever to see the Yankees return to dominance. From the outside, the hire looked like a bust, with headlines like "Clueless Joe" plastered all over the streets of New York and in the minds of fans.

Steinbrenner, as usual, reacted badly to the knee-jerk opinions of the New York media and, incredibly enough, was ready to move Torre to general manager (GM) and bring back Showalter as manager before the start of the 1996 season. But Showalter had already moved on from the Yankees, agreeing to a deal to manage the expansion Arizona Diamondbacks beginning in 1998. So, it was left to Torre to lead the team.

Inside the clubhouse, the players Torre would manage quickly found out just what type of person would lead them through that 1996 season and beyond. Torre, quite simply, was living on borrowed time professionally; he hadn't been sure he'd ever get a fourth shot at managing, and when that opportunity came, he became a manager who did his job without the fear of losing it.

---

[8] Prior to the 1996 season, Torre's regular-season managerial record stood at a woeful 894–1,003.

Steinbrenner had been indecisive in his search for a new leader and was now stuck with Torre. Torre was less intimidated by Steinbrenner's bullying than most managers who came before him. The fear of being fired was a classic Steinbrenner weapon that would quickly be disarmed because of the cool attitude of his new manager.

Players on the Yankees found Torre's quiet confidence and sincerity refreshing. He operated in a completely different manner than his predecessor; Showalter was tightly wound and had a controlling style that eventually wore on the team's veterans.

Torre's players would come to realize that their manager had a unique way of treating them. "What I try to do is treat everybody fairly," the manager once said. "It doesn't mean I treat everybody the same. But everybody deserves a fair shake. That's the right thing to do. I'd rather be wrong trusting somebody than never trusting them."

As a manager, Torre saw fit to give his players autonomy unless a crucial situation occurred. "When the rest of the team starts noticing things, you have to get this [situation] fixed," Torre stated. "That's my job. I like to give individuals what I believe is the room they need, but when I sense that other people are affected, team-wise, I have to find a solution to it and take an approach that is a little more serious."

From the outset in 1996, one of the best moves Torre made was the strategic assembling of a coaching staff. Once he was hired, Torre realized he had shortcomings as a manager, but he desperately wanted to win now that he'd been given a golden opportunity to do so in New York. Bringing in the right staff for support would help Torre accomplish his goals quicker, and he knew time was of the essence with the always unpredictable Steinbrenner looming above.

In his collection of coaches, Torre pieced together three people (Mel Stottlemyre, Chris Chambliss, and Willie Randolph) who had experience in New York and understood the demands of playing for the Yankees. He also brought in José Cardenal, a coaching veteran and outside influence, for a fresh perspective; and finally, Don Zimmer, also an outsider, was brought in as someone who had previously managed and had gone through the wringer much as Torre had. It was a beautiful sense of foresight, on Torre's part, to recognize that his best chance at making the most of this managerial opportunity was to surround himself with people who had experiences and strengths that he lacked at that point.

Addressing his players on the first day of spring training in 1996, Torre told them point-blank, "All of my coaches have been to the World Series. That's what I want. But I don't want to win just one. I want to win three of them in a row. I want to establish something here that's special. I don't want to sacrifice principles and players to do it one time. I want to establish a foundation to be the kind of ball club that is going to be able to repeat."

The foundation, the tone, and the vision for how this version of the Yankees would look had been set by Torre. Now it was up to him and his team to prove that they could accomplish what they set out to do: *WIN*.

Building Trust

Joe Torre's philosophy as a manager and leader of the Yankees followed a simple principle: *trust*. Torre is the son of an abusive father, and he had learned throughout his adult life how much the lack of trust between his father and the rest of his family led to unwanted stress, yelling, screaming, and crying.

Torre grew up to be a different type of man than his father. To build trust with his players, the manager made it clear from the onset that he would communicate with them first before anything reached the media. "I thought it was my obligation to communicate with them so they would have the information right from me," Torre explained of his relationship with his players. "My one point to the players was they were never going to read something that they haven't heard from me, at least something significant. And that's part of the trust I try to create."

In this approach, Torre's philosophies could not have been more different from that of someone like Billy Martin, who would use the media as a way to instigate players and show his superiority in the clubhouse. Torre wanted his players to look at one another in there or on the field and know that they had each other's backs.

One of the more memorable moments of the Torre tenure, testing the trust built between himself and his players, came on May 19, 1998, while playing in the Bronx versus the Baltimore Orioles. The Orioles were clinging to a slim lead late in the game when centerfielder Bernie Williams drilled a home run into the upper deck in right field, off pitcher Armando Benítez, giving the Yankees a 7–5 lead.

The Yankee Stadium crowd was buzzing, and on the next pitch, Benítez smoked first baseman Tino Martinez in the upper back with a fastball. As Martinez bent over in pain, both benches quickly cleared from their dugouts, with the Yankees' side led by one of their emotional leaders, left fielder Darryl Strawberry.

The two teams met at the pitcher's mound with some shouting, pushing, and shoving. The Yankee players were incensed at Benítez for his immaturity and for his dangerous pitch to Martinez. Then, running in from the outfield bullpen, Yankees pitchers Jeff Nelson and Graeme Lloyd got to Benítez through the pile of players on the mound and unloaded punches, starting off a brawl that lasted more than five minutes and almost became criminal after Strawberry attempted (but failed) to clock Benítez in the head near the top of the Orioles' dugout.

During the incident, Martinez was visibly irate, and in the visitor's dugout Torre pleaded desperately with Strawberry to go back to the Yankees' side before the veteran slugger caused more harm than had already happened. After the game, the Yankees remained unified, but they decided against future retaliation and more ugliness. The pitch by Benítez that hit Martinez was classless, the Orioles were embarrassed, and the Yankees' reaction was less than ideal. Torre's team had shown him that they had each other's backs in the worst of times; now it was time to get back to playing baseball.

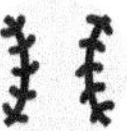

For much of the era, Torre and his Yankees operated in a more measured tone than they did during that game versus Baltimore in 1998. That was because the manager never made the Yankee players feel as if any particular game was bigger than any other. Torre always told his club that there was enough pressure in New York from fans and the media; they didn't need any added pressure from him.

"He was a manager I found easy to play for," said Torre's first catcher and future successor, Joe Girardi. "Not that I really found any managers hard to play for, but Joe had a calmness about him in a place that is not always so calm, and it made you feel like everything was going to be okay if we stuck together."

One of Torre's starting pitchers during the late 1990s was David Cone. Cone said of his manager, "You could sense that he was going to be a calming influence. He had a lot of experience." A starting pitcher for Torre from 2001 to 2007, Mike Mussina, added, "I always thought the personality of the team fed off of Joe Torre. And Joe was never too emotional either way, up or down. He trusted his players and trusted them to be ready."

Torre preferred to communicate in a low tone, and he did not want to challenge people as a fear tactic. But that didn't mean he *wouldn't* confront people if it was necessary, and he strongly believed that having difficult conversations with people was a better route than sweeping issues under the rug.

By ignoring something troublesome, Torre explained, he would have been crossing a line on accrued trust. "Even now I may have trouble when I have to tell someone the truth if it's not a pleasant thing, but I won't lie to them. I can't do that. The only way you get commitment is through trust, and you've got to try and earn that trust."

In her best-selling book, *Dare to Lead*, Brené Brown writes of trust, "It is earned not through heroic deeds, or even highly visible actions, but through paying attention, listening, and gestures of genuine care and connection." Torre was a master at all three of those leadership attributes, and he would let his players accept their hard-earned glory, while being able to deflect from them the harsh, even if sometimes warranted, criticisms from the press and fans.

Early in his tenure, Torre showed trust in his players by not playing favorites. After dropping the first two games of the 1996 World Series, Torre benched his starting first baseman, Tino Martinez, his starting third baseman, Wade Boggs, and his starting right fielder, Paul O'Neill, all of whom were struggling to produce at the plate. Cecil Fielder, Charlie Hayes, and Darryl Strawberry were inserted from the bench into those positions and made major contributions in the next four games of the series, all of which the Yankees won, with Hayes catching the final out of the final game.

It didn't matter to the manager that Martinez, Boggs, and O'Neill were the primary guys during the regular season—they weren't producing on the biggest stage, and baseball is as much of a business as it is a game. Torre's *job* was to win, but the decisions he made did not always sit well with his players. As a leader, some decisions will seem harsh no matter what the circumstances, even if they are for the betterment of the team.

Upon being released by the Yankees after the 1997 season, Fielder publicly ripped Torre for what he viewed as mishandling of his playing time during that season. The reality was that Fielder's competition, Tino Martinez, was in the midst of a breakout season in 1997. Martinez hit forty-four homers that year, made his first and only All-Star appearance with the Yankees, and finished second in the MVP voting. Torre couldn't have taken Martinez out of the lineup even if he wanted to.

Another harsh player decision by Torre came a few years later. With two outs in the fifth inning of Game 4 of the 2000 World Series, Torre removed starting pitcher Denny Neagle from the game with the New York Mets slugging catcher, Mike Piazza, due to hit; Piazza had crushed a long, two-run homer off Neagle in his previous at-bat and cut the Yankees' lead to 3–2. Torre didn't want to let Neagle face Piazza again, and clinging to a one-run lead, he pulled his starter, even though Neagle was one out away from qualifying for a win—his first World Series win—should the Yankees hang on to the lead and win the game.

The manager summoned out of the bullpen one of his most trusted assets, pitcher David Cone, to handle Piazza and any threat that the Mets would steal the game or the series. Cone got Piazza to fly out to end the inning, and the Yankees won the World Series in five games.

But after his early hook in Game 4, Neagle didn't hide his annoyance with the decision by Torre. "I'm still disappointed," the pitcher said. "Because you're a competitor, you want to be in those situations, and I feel confident in my ability to get out of those kind of situations. But, that's why the manager gets paid what he does, because he makes those decisions."

Neagle couldn't have said it better: in the heat of the moment, it was Torre who was being paid to make the big, in-game decision. At times, players can feel superhero-like and misread a situation in the midst of competition. A manager is there to provide a more objective and calm perspective, and that's exactly how Torre usually operated.

Torre was also keenly able to use his softer approach toward exercising trust. In 1998, Yankees second baseman Chuck Knoblauch was struggling mightily after demanding a trade from the Minnesota Twins that got him sent to New York in a blockbuster deal. Before the trade, Knoblauch was already a four-time All-Star, and he was considered around the league to be an above-average defender at second base, winning his first Gold Glove Award in 1997.

Now with the Yankees, prior to the All-Star break in 1998, Knoblauch had already made ten errors in the field. Compounding matters at the time was his father's struggle with Alzheimer's disease. Midway through the season, Knoblauch asked to talk with his manager.

In these types of situations, a person is lost, and what they're searching for may be an array of different elements, both professional and personal. A true leader will highlight success, in spite of everything that's dragging an individual down, and remind them of positive contributions they make.

That's precisely what Torre did for Knoblauch. First, Torre told his leadoff hitter that he had a high on-base percentage, he was extending at-bats and raising pitch counts for opposing pitchers, plus he was on a team setting a record pace for wins. Torre also related to Knoblauch, telling him of his own experience being traded to the St. Louis Cardinals from the Atlanta Braves prior to the 1969 season.

In one chat, Torre was able to validate Knoblauch's importance to the Yankees as well as relate to his personal vulnerabilities of being traded and being expected to produce immediately. The approach worked; Knoblauch would go on to make only three errors the rest of that season, and hit the game-tying three-run home run in Game 1 of the World Series.

Establishing a Working Relationship with a Difficult Boss

Trust was Torre's best attribute during his time as manager of the Yankees, because it gave him the ability to defuse George Steinbrenner and even build a decent working relationship with the Boss. In fact, the success of Torre's Yankees can be widely attributed to his rapport with Steinbrenner.

Prior to Torre, the Yankees had gone through eleven different managers since 1972. Torre would lead the Yankees for twelve seasons, with his teams winning four World Series championships, six American League pennants, and ten AL East division titles. Torre's clubs made the playoffs every season under his leadership, while averaging just under ninety-eight wins per season.

It's a myth to think that Torre and the Yankees waltzed through the dynasty years or bullied their way to four World Series titles. They dealt with the same type of frustrations from their people that many companies in the business world see on a daily basis: insecurity (Chuck Knoblauch), being too critical (Tino Martinez), neediness

(Paul O'Neill), and the overbearing imposition of an owner (Steinbrenner).

Before Torre came to the Yankees, he was acutely aware of the potential pitfalls he might face with the callous Steinbrenner. But the Boss's constant jabs, both in person and in the media, seemed to have no effect on Torre's quiet demeanor. The manager was able to carry that calmness into his clubhouse.

In an organization that had previously been anything but comfortable around Steinbrenner, the players finally began to see the side of the Boss that they would most appreciate: his extreme desire and willingness to win. For the first time ever, it seemed, there was a cohesiveness between the Yankees' players, their manager, and their owner. The results of the teams from that era speak for themselves.

While there were still times of discontent and frustration among the two, Torre came to most appreciate the accessibility of Steinbrenner, remembering that previous owners he had worked for were either absent from day-to-day operations or had the team in the lower rungs of multiple business priorities. Torre and Steinbrenner wanted to win above anything else, and even with their differing personalities and philosophies, they found a way to make the relationship work to the best of its ability for twelve years, for the betterment of the team.

Reflecting on that time period, there is no doubt that Torre was the leader the Yankees needed to be successful. His ability to deflect, defuse, and create a united front was instrumental in building a long-term *Culture of Excellence*.

The Transition of Joes: From Torre to Girardi

Joe Torre came to the Yankees during a time when they were oozing with on-field talent and had a hunger to recapture the winning legacy created by the franchise in the days of legendary players such as Babe Ruth, Lou Gehrig, Joe DiMaggio, and Mickey Mantle. Torre's teams responded with some astounding results: from 1996 through 2003, the Yankees averaged ninety-eight wins per season (more than sixty percent of games played), won sixteen of twenty postseason series in which they appeared, played in six World Series, won four championships, and came within three games of winning six titles in eight seasons.

Change was on the horizon, however, as the team failed to make it back to the World Series between 2004 and 2007. For years, there had been a growing tension among Torre, Steinbrenner, and the other Yankee executives, who wanted their manager to rely more on the growing analytics trend in baseball. There was also a sense that Torre was getting *too* casual in his day-to-day approach as a manager, although one could argue that he continued to make the playoffs even as his team aged and changed dramatically from the dynasty years, while the parity in baseball increased more than ever before. Nonetheless, Torre decided to leave the Yankees after they offered him a one-year $5 million contract for 2008, or $2.5 million less than he made in 2007.

Joe Girardi, a former player and a three-time world champion with the Yankees, beat out fan favorite former first baseman Don Mattingly and was named the thirty-second manager in team history on October 30, 2007. Girardi's return to the Yankees, this time as a manager, came during a period where the club's core players were severely aging, the Boss was no longer part of the day-to-day operations, and tensions at the executive level rivaled those that were the norm prior to Steinbrenner's second suspension in 1990.

If Girardi were going to succeed in New York, then *stability* would have to be his cornerstone ingredient. Although his predecessor's tenure as manager of the Yankees had lasted longer than anyone else's during the Steinbrenner era, Torre's time in New York ended bitterly after the Yankees were knocked out of the first round of the playoffs for the third consecutive season.

Girardi was ushered in to provide a fresh dose of cohesion and help calm the choppy waters. As a man, he was known as an over-preparer, but an individual who believed heavily in data. Girardi was ready to make the most of the information revolution in baseball, and upon getting the job with the Yankees he created a color-coded binder—known as "Girardi's Binder"—that was packed with matchups and Yankees' scouting notes.

The man, with his appetite for analytics, quickly proved himself to be masterful at using the Binder in his handling of the Yankees' bullpen. His first five teams finished in the top half in all of baseball in terms of earned run average (ERA). More importantly, he was able to maximize each reliever's value by using a rigorous rotation system that kept his relief pitchers fresh for the entire season. Girardi assigned his relievers to specific roles and situations in which they would appear, only veering from the norm when extenuating circumstances arose.

The Binder helped Girardi make a key decision for the offense during the Yankees' championship run in 2009. Early in that season, Girardi realized that his shortstop, Derek Jeter, was prone to hitting the ball on the ground, thus resulting in double plays being turned when center fielder, Johnny Damon, batting leadoff, would reach base ahead of Jeter. There was also the oddity of Damon being preceded in the lineup by left fielder Brett Gardner, another left-handed bat.

Balance is the key to a successful baseball lineup. Splitting up two left-handed batters at the bottom and the top of the batting order made it harder for opposing managers to leave in left-handed specialist pitchers because they would have to face a right-handed batter (Jeter) *in between* Gardner and then Damon.

The subtleties of baseball.

Girardi made a permanent change to the lineup early in 2009, slotting Jeter to the leadoff spot and dropping Damon right below, and it was a move that paid huge dividends. By slugging twenty-four home runs, Damon showed more power from the two-hole than he had in any season since 2006, and Jeter, at age thirty-five, batted .334, hit eighteen home runs, drove in sixty-six runners, and got on base in more than 40 percent of his plate appearances.

Analytics, it appeared, *was* the right direction to move toward.

Displaying Accountability

Joe Girardi can be described as hard-working, detail-oriented, loyal, and supportive. But even great leaders can have miscues. What's important is *how* the leader reacts when they make a mistake. Girardi highlighted his ability to hold himself culpable during one of the tensest managing moments of his Yankees career.

In Cleveland in 2017, down one game to none in the best-of-five series versus the defending American League champion Indians, the Indians sent up pinch hitter Lonnie Chisenhall with two outs and two on in the bottom of the sixth inning, and the Yankees up 8–3. Yankees pitcher Chad Green pumped a fastball, up and in, on Chisenhall, and the ball struck the bottom knob of his bat, which should have constituted a foul ball. Instead, the home plate umpire signaled for Chisenhall to take first base, believing the ball had nicked the pinch hitter's hand and *not* the knob of the bat.

Intensifying the situation was the fact that the foul tip had occurred on an 0–2 pitch from Green, and catcher Gary Sánchez, not always known for his defensive strengths, caught the foul ball—thus, Chisenhall would have been out on strikes and the inning would have been over.

Hit-by-pitch calls *are* reviewable under Major League Baseball's replay rules, but Girardi never issued a challenge, even after his catcher and pitcher pleaded from the field for there to be one. Girardi later said that the Yankees ran out of time to issue the replay challenge, and before anyone could fully grasp what was happening that night in Cleveland, Francisco Lindor stepped to the plate and drilled a grand-slam home run to cut the lead to 8–7. The Indians later won the game in the thirteenth inning, and the Yankees were on the brink of elimination, down two games to none in a best-of-five series.

After the Game 2 loss, Girardi was, predictably, roasted by the press, social media, and fans for his decision *not* to challenge the Chisenhall "foul tip." The manager faced the press, took responsibility for his decisions, and did his best to tame the wildfire that was blazing as the Yankees' season appeared to quickly be coming to an end.

It's one matter to be accountable in public—an important attribute for any leader—but it's even more imperative to be willing to accept responsibility for *all* decisions within private confines. Describing the scene after the Game 2 ALDS blunder, then-shortstop Didi Gregorius said of his manager, "He talked to us for a little bit, had a quick meeting. He admitted to it. It just shows that everybody is united. Everybody has accountability.

"That's the best thing," Gregorius continued. "If you made a mistake, you admit it. You pass it on. That's in the past. All he told us was, 'Hey, let's play one game at a time right now, and that's all we can control right now.' Whatever happened in the past happened in the past. We as a team, we always have each other's back."

Their manager demonstrated a humility that showed he cared more about the team than about saving face, and the Yankees responded to Girardi and the adversity by winning the next three games, advancing to the American League Championship Series versus the Houston Astros. It's a comeback that's still talked about as one of the first sparks of the new Yankees' core, and without Girardi's professionalism, the current group of players may have flamed out before they even had a chance to get hot.

Treating People with Respect

"I believe that this game is really hard," Girardi once said. "And players know when they screwed up, and you don't need to publicly talk about it. It's already bad enough. So, if you have to take a bullet, you take it, because I always tell people I know what really happened. I do. But I don't want players to ever feel embarrassed. I think that's the hardest part of the game when you feel embarrassed. Because you're going to be hard enough on yourself."

Being a former player, Girardi understood the strenuous lives led by baseball players. "The one thing that I think is important for a manager is that the players know that you care but also never forget how hard it is to play the game," Girardi explained. "The effort is there all the time, but sometimes it just doesn't happen. Some day a guy gets three hits, and he's going to take the same approach the next day. It doesn't happen, and that's why there is a human element of the game."

Mark Teixeira, Girardi's first baseman for eight seasons from 2009 to 2016, thought his manager thoroughly understood that the Yankee players were more than *just* ballplayers. "I've always said that I respect that Joe cares for me more as a man than he does about me as a baseball player. Because he knows how hard it is to play the game. He knows there is a lot of failure involved. It's more important that we are comfortable with him as a man.

"He cares about our families, because if that's taken care of, it makes [our time] on the field easier. Knowing how he cares about us as men, as husbands, as fathers, that allows us to do our job on the field."

Making Difficult Decisions

After the Yankees missed the playoffs in 2008, ownership responded by acquiring top-level free agents, pitchers CC Sabathia and AJ Burnett, and first baseman Mark Teixeira. The moves represented a quick fix to bolster the team's chances in 2009 and beyond, with ownership spending $423.5 million that off-season just on the three superstars. The splurge coincided with the grand opening of the new Yankee Stadium—the state-of-the-art $1.5 *billion* cathedral bearing its predecessor's name.

For their efforts, the organization was rewarded with a World Series championship in 2009, number twenty-seven in franchise history. The Yankees returned to the playoffs in each of the next three seasons but failed to make it back to the World Series, and by the time the 2013 campaign began, their core of players was again beginning to show cracks.

Mariano Rivera, arguably the greatest relief pitcher in the history of the game, announced that he would be retiring after the 2013 season. Rivera pitched brilliantly during his swan season, but injuries ravaged core, everyday players—including their captain, Derek Jeter, and the melodramatic slugger, Alex Rodriguez.

Girardi's job was significantly changing, and the manager had to innovate to find ways to get the Yankees' aging players in games, but also keep them fresh enough so that they wouldn't break down over the course of a 162-game season. Oh, and he also had to keep the organizational mandate of moving forward and competing for a championship.

Further complicating the glaring aging problem for the Yankees' players was the fact that Girardi had also *played* with core members. He was now tasked with difficult decisions on playing time and how to best use former everyday players in a reduced role.

Predictably, the results were mixed. In 2014, Girardi refused to move Jeter down from his leadoff spot in the lineup, even though the shortstop had the fewest hits and the lowest on-base percentage of any full season of his career. If Jeter wasn't getting on base, then he wasn't scoring runs (he would score the lowest number of runs of any full season in his career), and as a result, the Yankees weren't scoring as many runs as they had in the past, which ultimately led to fewer wins. The eighty-four wins for the Yankees in 2014 was the lowest number for the franchise in any full season since 1992 (and four years before Jeter's rookie campaign), when they won only seventy-six games and had their last losing season.

Before the Jeter dilemma, there was a fairly public feud between Girardi and Jorge Posada, the catcher who took over for Girardi in New York after the 1999 season. As is detailed in his autobiography, *The Journey Home: My Life in Pinstripes*, Posada claimed there was a "lack of respect" and "bad communication" directed at him from Girardi. Further frustration from Posada came as a result of being stripped of his catcher position and transitioned to a full-time designated hitter (DH) in 2011, which would turn out to be the final season of his career.

In what had to be another difficult decision-making process, Girardi had to decide how to keep the team competitively moving forward, while also taking into consideration the feelings of a player who had heavily contributed to the last four World Series titles. It was not an easy moment in Girardi's tenure, but he held firm in his belief that Posada better helped the Yankees as a DH. Posada's replacement that year as catcher, Russell Martin, was an All-Star, played brilliant defense behind home plate, and belted eighteen home runs.

Yankees History Lesson: 2013–2017

Through all of the difficulties, Girardi was able to do some of his best managing from 2013 to 2016. He remained masterful at handling the veteran roster and kept the Yankees in playoff contention until the final weeks of each season in 2013, 2014, and 2016. His best squad during that four-year stretch, in 2015, won eighty-seven games and qualified for the playoffs, but the season ended quietly in October after a Wild Card Game loss at Yankee Stadium to the Houston Astros.

During these lean years, it became more apparent than ever that the structure of the game no longer allowed the Yankees to freely outspend all of the other teams in the open market. It was a humbling period in franchise history, one in which they had to learn how to rebuild with player development, rather than constantly reload with free agents.

Never one to make excuses, Girardi seemed to grasp just how challenging it was to win a World Series. "You realize how tough it is," he explained after an empty season for the Yankees. "That's the one thing you realize, how difficult it is to win a World Series. There are so many things that have to happen. You start in spring training, you play thirty games there, you play 162 games in the regular season, and it is difficult when it ends too abruptly, because any team that gets in the playoffs really believes they can win the World Series."

By the time the 2017 season rolled around, it was abundantly clear that the franchise was once again at a crossroads. The Yankees' GM, Brian Cashman, had been stressing the importance of making the roster younger and more flexible, a by-product of—and necessity to compete within—the confines of the current collective bargaining agreement (CBA). He was also trying to rid the team of large contracts that resulted in the Yankees paying money to everyone else in baseball due to an element called the "luxury tax"— and these were aspects the George Steinbrenner regime never had to deal with.

"The Yankees have acted a certain way for a long time," Cashman said of the decrepit Yankee strategy. "And trying to change course from that was difficult. But at the same time, it's continuing to remind everybody that the chess board that we're playing is way different than the one their [Hal and Hank Steinbrenner's] dad was playing.

"They have limitations on the international amateur space," Cashman continued. "They have limitations in the domestic amateur space, they have penalties on winning, and a significant portion now is the luxury tax and revenue sharing."

At the 2016 trade deadline, Cashman got approval from Hal Steinbrenner, the current owner of the Yankees, to execute a "soft" sell-off. The last time the team "sold" was, ironically, in 1989, when the Yankees traded Ricky Henderson to the Oakland Athletics.

Steinbrenner wanted to remain competitive, but he also came to understand the significant value his top players had. In the closing days before the trade deadline, it was clear that the Yankees had to do something different if they wanted to play competitive baseball in the future. Accelerating the youth movement that began in 2015 was the top priority *and* of greater importance than winning the 2016 World Series.

In a string of moves that can be described as both brilliant and lucky, Cashman stripped the Yankees of top-tier players that ate up a large chunk of the team's payroll,[9] and also executed smaller, but still impactful, trades.[10] In return, the Yankees received blue-chip prospects,[11] and in a twenty-four-hour period the Yankees went from

---

[9] Aroldis Chapman was dealt to the Chicago Cubs, and Andrew Miller was traded to the Cleveland Indians.

[10] Carlos Beltrán was moved to the Texas Rangers, and Iván Nova was sent to Pittsburgh to play for the Pirates.

[11] Gleyber Torres from the Cubs and Clint Frazier from the Indians.

being one of the oldest teams in the majors to one of the youngest, and their minor league system went from being one of the worst in baseball to one of the best.

Regardless of the organizational ramifications, the clubhouse reaction to the trades was not good. Mark Feinsand, a reporter for MLB.com, tweeted on the day of the trade deadline, "Yankees clubhouse is dead silent this morning. Feels like a funeral." This reception to trades is predictable in most major league clubhouses, but especially so in New York, where the expectation to win is as sky-high as the Empire State Building. So, to temper the feelings, Cashman shored up the Yankees' bullpen for the rest of 2016 in case of a late playoff push.[12]

As a result of the 2016 sell-off, the Yankees were not expected to compete in 2017, even after a late push was spurred on by another injection of the youth movement—most notably the home run barrage produced by catcher Gary Sánchez, who almost won Rookie of the Year, even though he only played in fifty-three games in 2016.

But, again, New York is a different animal when it comes to expectations and how the Yankees operate. Girardi summed it up well: "Brian [Cashman] and his staff and the organization are trying to put this team in a good position to have a long run of not just playing well, but winning championships. It's not about being a second Wild Card team and winning one game, or losing one game. We want to win championships."

The "Baby Bombers," as they were known in 2017, took the baseball world by surprise and won ninety-one games en route to a Wild Card Game victory versus the Minnesota Twins. Then they produced an ALDS upset of the heavily favored and defending-league champion, Cleveland Indians. Finally, they were ousted by the eventual champs, the Houston Astros, in a thrilling seven-game ALCS.

----

[12] Adding pitchers Tyler Clippard and Adam Warren, among others.

For all of the success of 2017 and the high ceiling that remained, friction lingered between the Yankees' front office and their manager. Girardi, for all his positives, had an extreme inability to *relax*. While manager of the Yankees, he would consistently work fifteen-hour days, and sometimes even longer, while navigating through a very strict and regimented daily schedule.

It's hard to find time for fun when your schedule is jammed to the minute each day. It's even more difficult to find time for *connection*. Joe Torre was a master at understanding and connecting with his players, while Girardi routinely struggled to understand any lifestyle other than his own. In 2017, Girardi was leading a group of players younger than at any point in his Yankee tenure, and it seemed more and more likely that his inability to loosen up would ultimately cost him his job.

Failure to Communicate

Six days after the Yankees lost to the Astros in 2017, Girardi was informed by the Yankees' brass that his services were no longer needed. He won the World Series in 2009 and finished his Yankee tenure with a regular-season record of 910–710. But Girardi's intense and passionate traits clouded his ability to unwind and grasp the thrilling opportunity it is to run one of the world's greatest organizations.

The fierce, and sometimes harsh, attitude that Girardi often displayed was beginning to erode his relationships with his younger players—players that the Yankees had invested a lot of time and effort into, as they were regarded as the future of the club. If the Baby Bombers were having difficulties meshing with their manager, then that was reason enough for the organization to decide to split ways with Girardi. The decision to move on from their tenured manager was one that was two to three years in the making, with Cashman voicing doubts that Girardi's "clenched fist intensity" would be the best fit for a young roster.

The disconnect between Girardi and his players took center stage in August of 2017, when the manager publicly called out the poor defense of his second-year catcher, Gary Sánchez, saying Sánchez needed "to improve, bottom line." Sánchez was subsequently benched, which seemed out of place, because Girardi usually went the extra mile to defend his players from outside criticism and internal embarrassment.

So, it was left to Cashman, who recommended to Hal Steinbrenner that they allow Girardi's contract to expire. Cashman delivered the news to Girardi that he would not be retained as manager, telling Girardi that they needed a leader who better understood the younger players, and overwhelmingly, Girardi was not that person.

After ten seasons at the helm, Joe Girardi was out of work, and the Yankees were on the hunt for only their second manager in the past twenty-two seasons—pretty good for a franchise that had burned through twenty different managers between 1973 and 1992.

Now Managing for the Yankees, Aaron "Bleeping" Boone

Joe Girardi's successor in the manager's seat would be a man even further off the radar for hire than Joe Torre prior to 1996, but like Torre, he was a deft *relationship builder*. Aaron Boone was introduced as the thirty-third manager of the Yankees on December 6, 2017.

Boone had never managed a game in his life and came to the Yankees after spending several seasons as a broadcaster in multiple capacities with ESPN. The new manager *was* a baseball lifer, though; his own career spanned thirteen years, and his grandfather, father, and brother all played in the big leagues.[13] Boone also hit one of the most famous home runs in Yankees history: a walk-off solo homer in

------

[13] Ray, Bob, and Bret Boone.

Game 7 of the 2003 Championship Series versus the hated Boston Red Sox.

There was a high risk associated with hiring a person who had never managed or coached at any level in baseball. But the Yankees' front office strongly felt that Boone's ability to blend the analytics revolution with his relationship-building skills was the recipe to help them attain their ultimate goal of a championship.

In his opening press conference, Boone showed his keen understanding of the situation he was being thrust into, saying coolly but confidently, "I understand what the expectations are."

Brian Cashman praised Boone's intelligence, open-mindedness, and communication skills as having been factors in the Yankees' decision to hire the rookie manager.

Hal Steinbrenner also had high praise for his new manager. "His calmness, patience, confidence, I think with a young team that's only going to get younger … he's going to be good for this particular group at this particular time."

Steinbrenner's words highlight a key point: There are various reasons why people in positions of leadership get relieved of their duties. Girardi struggled to connect to younger players, and so the Yankees let him go, knowing they had a budding core that would be in place for years to come. Boone was brought in to be the manager for the team as it's constructed *right now*, and there's a chance that somewhere down the road the "fit" won't be as good as it looks now. To this extent, it's important to remember that one's ability to successfully lead is highly dependent on circumstances.

Boone knew why he was selected for New York, saying, "I feel like my job is getting the most out of these players, especially the younger players."

Another reason Boone was brought in was for his calm demeanor. In this way he, again, is more like a Joe Torre than Joe Girardi. Connecting with people is Boone's biggest strength, but he is also an adept tension diffuser, saying, "If all you're gonna do is worry about results, you'll just play tight and lose."

Boone wants his players to consume metrics, sharpen their mechanics, take care of their body between starts, and most importantly, *play the game and let the competition decide.* It's not a sexy daily mantra, like Mariano Duncan's famous 1996, "We play today, we win today, das it," but it seems to fit the calm atmosphere that Boone has created in the Yankees' clubhouse.

Boone, like Torre, should be considered a hire from "the outside." It's true that Boone is forever immortalized in one of the greatest moments in Yankees history, but his playing career in New York ended quickly and bitterly. After being traded to the Yankees in July of 2003, and hitting the famous home run that October, Boone was unceremoniously released after blowing out his knee playing pickup basketball in January of 2004, gone before he could soak in the royal treatment from Yankee fans for his October heroics.

The unfortunate injury situation from Boone's playing days seemed to be in the rearview mirror of Yankees executives—and considered a *learning experience* for the new manager, if you will. The Yankees saw in Boone a person who knew how to handle the media, someone who had played and succeeded under New York's brightest lights, and an individual who was the best fit to take over the millennial wave of Yankee players.

The manager flexed his marvelous communication skills often during his first season in New York, but no situation may have been more important than his skillful handling of Aroldis Chapman's knee issues. Chapman was sidelined for much of the second half of 2018 with knee inflammation, and although he returned in mid-September for the Yankees' regular-season stretch run, he wasn't his old self.

Knowing that he would hurt his team's chances of reaching the playoffs by pitching poorly, Chapman asked his manager to ease him back into game flow by keeping him out of his primary pitching role. Instead of telling the full account to the media, Boone—knowing very well what stories would come of it—decided to say that it was his staff's decision to hold back on using Chapman in his customary position. Just like that, the non-story stayed that way. The manager prevented the situation from becoming a distraction, simply by communicating and understanding the player.

If there was ever going to be consensus that Aaron Boone was the right hire for the Yankees, the concrete evidence would come in the form of the 2019 season, a season where the team was destroyed by injuries to many of their core players.

Boone, with the help of his player leaders, set the tone and clearly defined what the expectations of the full active roster would be. In the first meeting of 2019, during spring training, the Yankees' established players stood in front of the room and delivered their "next man up" message: "We said, 'Hey, everyone in this room could get used,'" Aaron Judge recalled. "It doesn't matter if it's April, September, whenever. Everyone can play, be part of this team at some point, and just be ready for your opportunities.

"To see not just one guy step up, but another guy and another guy and another guy? Everyone's really rallied around that."

Of course, it's one thing to say "be ready to play;" it's another to produce when called upon. Why does the manager think that his squad is remarkably successful and resilient?

"I think it's not just brought a level of physical toughness to the room, but it's forced guys to be mentally tough as well," Boone said of the Yankees' punishing 2019 season.

"I think it's part of the hunger that exists with those guys because they have the mindset that nothing's gonna get in my way, and nothing's gonna stop us, they all kinda pull for each other and know that the next guy is expected to do the job."

It remains to be seen if Boone can lead the Yankees to a championship, much less multiple titles. His competition in Boston, Alex Cora,[14] also a first-time manager, led the Boston Red Sox to a

---

[14] Cora's tenure in Boston will always be clouded by sign-stealing accusations while he was manager of the Red Sox from 2018 to 2020, and before that while the bench coach for the Houston Astros in 2017.

historic regular season in 2018 *and* the franchise's fourth World Series title since 2004. Boone's squads have won 100 regular-season games or more in 2018 and 2019, but fell short of a championship each time, losing in the playoffs to the Red Sox in 2018, and again to the Houston Astros in 2019.

Upon taking the job with no experience, Boone was (and remains) an easy target for scrutiny. His in-game decisions during the 2018 playoffs versus the Red Sox made it seem that he was too slow to react in a high-leverage and elimination-type situation. In the 2019 playoffs, he countered with lightning-quick adjustments to his starting pitchers, and replaced them with his powerful bullpen arms, but his offense let him down by not coming through with timely hits.

Boone can also come off as more "Joe Cool" than "Bronx Zoo," and fair or not, while Billy Martin-type outbursts are often overstated, they are used in part to judge a manager's competence. Thus, his "savages in that box" comments during a game on July 18, 2019, endeared him to fans, but also showed a fire burning within Boone that wasn't on display during his freshman campaign in 2018.

The modern game wants managers who are fluent in the role that analytics plays in decision making, which defines Aaron Boone as a leader and a facilitator. With Boone's slick approach toward leading, the Yankees should be a contender for the foreseeable future. The Yankees have once again proven that they know how to hire the *right people* for the *right job* in the *right situation.*

Summary of *The Manager's Seat*

Being the manager of any team is a difficult task. Too many people make assumptions about what they would do in a given situation without actually knowing the inner workings. Managers will always be under the microscope and scrutinized for their decisions. As a result, it is required that great managers—amazing leaders—have conviction and have the ability to sell people on what's best for them as individuals *and* as a team. If people believe in the manager, they will play and work harder, and they will buy into whatever concept of culture is being created.

Joe Torre, Joe Girardi, and Aaron Boone have all shown incredible leadership attributes during their time as manager of the Yankees. *Each person acted on their strengths as individuals and did not try to be someone they weren't.* Where they had weaknesses, each manager often relied on the help of their coaching staff and front office, exhibiting the ability to be fully self-aware in all circumstances.

Torre, Girardi, and Boone are not people without flaws, but overwhelmingly, collectively, they have been model leaders for their teams, and the entire Yankee organization, significantly enhancing the franchise's *Culture of Excellence*.

Chapter Three

Evil Empire Architects[15]

oday's baseball teams are all about collaboration. There are data people, the on-field manager, coaches, the scouting department, and the players themselves, and they are all part of the design put together by the most important part of any business: owners and front-office executives. It wasn't long ago that executives in baseball were a collection of former players and coaches. But since the beginning of the new millennium, there has been a seismic shift toward analytics, leading to a boom of a highly educated front-office staff ready to make significant changes.

The modern game, on the field, is all about playing the odds, while the game off the field is full of savvy individuals becoming more risk-averse and obsessed with value. Theo Epstein, now the Chicago Cubs' president, was one of the early information-age pioneers. Epstein grew up a Boston Red Sox fan, and after graduating from Yale University in 1995, he took a public relations internship with the San Diego Padres. By 2002 he was the Padres' director of baseball operations and quickly established himself as someone who understood that the future of the game lay in data-driven decisions.

Prior to the 2003 season, Epstein took over as general manager of the Red Sox. In 2004, he delivered the franchise its first World Series

---

[15] In this case, "architect" refers to the people who design and assemble a baseball team.

title since 1918, ending an eighty-six-year drought better known as "The Curse of the Bambino." After Epstein left Boston for the Chicago Northside in 2011, he helped assemble the roster that won the Cubs their first championship since 1908—ending another dry spell, known as "The Curse of the Billy Goat," in 2016.

Epstein's success helped pave the way for more individuals like him to be major stakeholders. As the years passed, there were fewer intuitive thoughts and decisions happening in baseball, and more emphasis being placed on data and analytics. Baseball lifers can (and have) adapted to this type of thought process, but it was the Ivy League types who revolutionized the sport forever, making it imperative to have a collaborative front office that runs with the efficiency of a retail store during the holiday rush.

Yankees Overview: 1984–1998

The power framework for the New York Yankees was *never* collaborative during the early days of the George Steinbrenner regime. Prior to his second suspension, Steinbrenner used intimidation to get what he wanted from his management personnel and the Yankee players. Steinbrenner would periodically bash his players, both privately in the clubhouse and very publicly in the newspaper. The Boss seemed to thrive on confrontation, and he was once quoted as saying, "When you take your boss on publicly, you can't just get away with it."

A lack of collaboration is hardly exclusive to Steinbrenner and the Yankees. In 2015, Jerry Dipoto, at the time the GM of the Los Angeles Angels, resigned in fury and rage over a clash in ideological differences with longtime Angels manager, Mike Scioscia. When Dipoto took over in 2011, he quickly revamped the franchise's front office, putting a much heavier emphasis on statistical data and advanced analytics. But the lack of support from Scioscia—who was more of an old-school baseball leader—made it impossible for Dipoto to effectively do his job or to find any happiness in it.

The disconnect between Steinbrenner and his on-field leaders was at its max in the 1980s. Yankees legend Yogi Berra was managing the team in 1984, leading them to a respectable 87–75 record. Despite the modest success, as a manager, Berra was always going to be in a tough spot around his ruthless owner. The former Yankees catcher had won ten championships as a player and another three as a coach,[16] yet he may as well have been a rookie in Class-A ball when it came to dealing with Steinbrenner.

Once, in a memorable and foul-mouthed tirade, Berra stood up to the Boss after Steinbrenner complained of ineptitude from the players. "I've had enough of this shit!" Berra stated. "You keep saying this is my team? That's a fucking lie and you know it! This is your fucking team.

"You put this fucking team together," the incensed Berra continued. "You make all the fucking moves around here. You get all the fucking players nobody else wants. You put this fucking team together and then you sit around and wait for us to lose so you can blame everybody else because you're a chickenshit fucking liar!"

This author often wonders if that moment was in the back of Steinbrenner's mind in 1985 when he unceremoniously fired Berra after only sixteen games.

When Steinbrenner was suspended in 1990, former Yankees player, coach, and scout, Gene Michael, took over as GM. His mission was simple: transform the organization. Team construction was the one aspect he would have complete control over during Steinbrenner's absence.

By 1993, the only big-name player who remained in New York from when Steinbrenner was suspended was first baseman Don Mattingly. During that time, Michael brought in other big-name acquisitions such as Jimmy Key and Wade Boggs. He also traded

---

[16] Berra played in parts of eighteen seasons with the Yankees from 1946 to 1963, and then appeared in four games for the crosstown-rival Mets in 1965. He also managed the Yankees during two separate stints—1964, and then from 1984 through the first sixteen games of 1985—while between his Yankee stints managing the Mets from 1972 until he was fired in August of 1975.

players with large salaries to recover some payroll flexibility. Most importantly, Michael allowed younger players to develop and contribute, like Bernie Williams—a cornerstone player on the dynasty teams in the late 1990s.

It has been said by many baseball people that Michael was *always* talking about his minor leaguers and the contributions they would one day make in the big leagues. Prior to Steinbrenner's 1990 suspension, these prospects-turned-professionals would have been cut or traded long before getting the chance to play in the Bronx. A classic Steinbrenner policy was to trade unproven prospects for already validated ballplayers.

Michael had a different rebuilding approach, and it was rooted in philosophies he displayed to the Boss back in the 1970s. He found left-handed batters—like Boggs and Paul O'Neill—to take advantage of Yankee Stadium's short porch in right field,[17] and he wanted disciplined hitters who would improve the team's on-base percentage.

Michael's approach proved wise, as the Yankees returned to postseason play in 1995 for the first time since 1981. But after a heartbreaking loss in the first round of the playoffs, Steinbrenner flexed his muscles, parting ways with manager Buck Showalter and demoting Michael to a scouting position. Replacing Michael was Houston Astros' GM Bob Watson, who, like many other people before him, probably saw the opportunity to build a championship-winning team in New York as a dream come true.

Watson accomplished that goal when the Yankees took home the title in 1996, which was the first for the franchise since 1978. But by the end of the 1997 season, Watson was convinced that the worst job in the world belonged to the GM of the New York Yankees—in other words, him. Steinbrenner had stopped communicating with Watson, and the Boss was turning to Michael for advice on trades and player evaluations or going to his player-development people in Tampa.

____

[17] A batter only needs to hit the ball 314 feet down the right field line at Yankee Stadium, making it one of the more hitter-friendly ballparks in the game.

Watson only heard from Steinbrenner when something went wrong—a typical pattern between Steinbrenner and his GMs.

In February of 1998, Watson finally reached his limit for tolerating Steinbrenner's demands, and he submitted his resignation letter just before the start of spring training. Before he officially cleaned out his office, Watson recommended to the Boss that he strongly consider a young man named Brian Cashman to take over as GM.

Cashman was a Yankee lifer—he had started his career with the organization as an eighteen-year-old intern in 1986, and after graduating from The Catholic University of America, he came onto the payroll as a part-time assistant GM. Steinbrenner took Watson's advice, and when Cashman took over as the Yankees' GM in February of 1998 he was, at age thirty, the second youngest person in that position in the history of baseball.

The newly appointed Cashman wasn't exactly thrilled about taking over the only organization he'd known in his professional career. "If you worked for the Yankees and saw what I saw," he once said, "the last thing you'd want is to be the GM."

But Cashman *was* the right man at the right time for the job. Buster Olney wrote in his bestseller, *The Last Night of the Yankees Dynasty*, that Cashman was "a perfect general manager for Steinbrenner because he had been trained by the organization, knew Steinbrenner's expectations, and could at least attempt to anticipate what Steinbrenner might need."

Being Bold: The Start of the Brian Cashman Era

The Boss was hungry for another championship in 1998. The Yankees had taken a step back in 1997, finishing second in the American League East but grabbing the Wild Card before falling to the Cleveland Indians in five games during the American League Division Series.

They were looking for a spark, and Brian Cashman promptly flexed his GM muscles, pulling off a blockbuster trade with the

Minnesota Twins that meant giving up three of the Yankees' top prospects but, in return, receiving the perennial All-Star second baseman and leadoff hitter, Chuck Knoblauch.

The hefty price of getting Knoblauch paid immediate dividends: The second baseman stole 31 bases, scored 117 runs, and most importantly, allowed everyone else in the lineup to find their proper spot below him. The biggest beneficiary of the move was Derek Jeter, who slotted into the two-hole of the lineup and hit .324 while scoring 124 runs and finishing third in the AL Most Valuable Player voting.

The 1998 New York Yankees won 114 times, then a regular-season record,[18] before capturing eleven more wins in the playoffs en route to the franchise's twenty-fourth World Series championship.

Cashman had proven himself to be a savvy GM, one who could build a championship-caliber team, and more importantly, one who could *manage a coexisting relationship with Steinbrenner.*

"He [Cashman] and George would have scream festivals for *hours,*" according to Jean Afterman, the assistant GM of the Yankees. "I'd close my door but could hear them down the hall. Brian backs down from no one—that's why George loved him."

Cashman would have to be strong-willed and patient to withstand and work for Steinbrenner for more than one season.

Prior to Cashman taking over as GM, the Yankees had operated with little regard for organizational structure. One of his early projects was to bridge the gap between the powers that be in New York and Tampa. Sure, there was a formal organizational chart, but nothing could stop Steinbrenner from making unilateral decisions during his heyday. It was the Boss's team, and it was his money being invested in all parts of the Yankees.

Cashman wanted the New York and Tampa bases to work together. He wanted there to be a healthy debate between the two camps, and ultimately, he wanted a unanimous decision to be made by all parties before bringing any recommendations to Steinbrenner.

---

[18] The Yankees' 1998 record was broken in 2001 by the Seattle Mariners, who won 116 regular-season games.

All of Cashman's early efforts in building an alliance between the New York and Tampa camps proved effective with the on-field product. Between 1998 and 2005, the Yankees made the playoffs each season by winning their division, and they won three straight World Series titles from 1998 to 2000.

After the title run ended in 2000, while they continued to win in the regular season, they were much less successful in the postseason. They blew a ninth-inning lead to the Arizona Diamondbacks in Game 7 of the 2001 World Series, which ended their consecutive title streak at three. Then they lost to the Florida Marlins in the 2003 World Series, a series in which they were heavily favored, but came out completely flat after the emotionally draining American League Championship Series dogfight with the Red Sox.

In 2004, the Yankees infamously became the first in baseball history to blow a three-games-to-none lead in the best-of-seven playoff series. They had to watch in shock as the Red Sox celebrated their ALCS victory on the Yankee Stadium infield before going on to win the World Series—the first for Boston since 1918.

The Boss's health began to seriously deteriorate in 2003, shortly before the start of the World Series, and by 2004 Steinbrenner was desperate for a championship. Knowing that his mortality was on the line, he began reverting to old habits. Where once there was a healthy debate between the full body of the front office, it now seemed obvious that all decisions regarding the organization reflected what Steinbrenner wanted.

He was signing players without input from Cashman, and he put great stress on the Yankees' payroll by giving out contracts that resulted in gobs of money being spent. The Yankees also began to decimate their farm system, trading young (and more affordable) assets for proven, but costly (and older), major league talent. Combine all of that with the increasing power struggle between New York and Tampa headquarters, and the Yankees were one disastrous move away from returning to their irrelevance of the 1980s.

To this point, Cashman had endured years of fifteen-hour days at Yankee Stadium and had dealt with Steinbrenner calling during and after the games, as well as late at night, complaining that the Yankees weren't good enough. Cashman was taught by Gene Michael to convey his feelings and fight for what he thought was right. By 2005, Cashman was convinced the franchise was at a crossroads and there was only one way to fix it, saying, "There's got to be a chain of command from the owner to the GM to the manager with nobody in between."

At one point prior to 2005, it was reported that Cashman told Steinbrenner, after one of his contracts expired, that he intended to leave the Yankees because of the disorganization in the baseball operations hierarchy. The threat of Cashman leaving to build a powerhouse team with another baseball organization, coupled with Steinbrenner's weakened health, set the stage for a new era in Yankees baseball.

After finishing negotiations with Steinbrenner, Cashman was given a three-year contract extension after the 2005 season, in which he gained additional clout by becoming the head of baseball operations. His growing influence within the Yankees' hierarchy was becoming clear.

This breakthrough for Cashman marked the end of George Steinbrenner's run as the unquestioned decision-maker of the New York Yankees, and the GM's continued body of work has given him credibility and value that make him one of the most indispensable people within the organization.

Understanding Internal Development

The office of Brian Cashman is, in a word, unique. His post has one wall with windows facing the stadium, two walls that are filled with the rosters of every big-league team, and a fourth wall that lists every player in the Yankees' organization with their salaries, service time, and age. These walls hold the formulas to the Yankees' success, and it all starts with *player development*.

When Cashman negotiated his contract to stay with the Yankees after 2005, he bargained with George Steinbrenner to give him money to build a mental-skills unit. The addition of such an investment was indicative of Cashman's foresight into the changing landscape of the game.

Billy Beane, the marvelous executive vice president of baseball operations for the Oakland Athletics, once said of his rival GM, "He [Cashman] knew there was no way to outspend teams forever and just wanted to be efficient." If the Yankees could no longer outspend everyone and win, then they needed to be better at scouting and developing their own players.

When the 2006 season started, it was obvious that Cashman's Yankees would look very different from past ones. Cashman reintroduced *youth* to the ball club: Chien-Ming Wang was permanently thrust into the starting rotation. He responded by delivering a stellar season and finished second in that season's Cy Young Award voting. A year after finishing second in the Rookie of the Year voting, second baseman Robinson Canó continued to establish himself as one of the game's brightest up-and-coming stars as he earned his first All-Star appearance.

The youth movement and increased level of influence that Cashman formed would not come without growing pains. Cashman had a strong desire to join the likes of Oakland in the new information revolution, but his manager, Joe Torre, hadn't fully warmed up to the idea. During his tenure as manager, Torre merely saw numbers as one device in the toolbox, not as a full-fledged philosophy.

The difference of opinions resulted in the first major clash between manager and GM during their time working together and signaled that the end of Torre's time in New York might not be that far off. The gap between the two men would only grow over the next couple of seasons.

Torre had once told Cashman to never forget that there was a heartbeat in the game of baseball, but Cashman's feeling at the time was that the organization needed a manager who was more analytical and relied less on intuition. Although it was reported that Steinbrenner wanted Torre back, one can conclude that Cashman was happy to see the famed manager take his talents to Los Angeles, opening the door further for the Yankees to continue building their own analytical cultural revolution.

Being Unafraid to Have Difficult Conversations

Brian Cashman was not afraid to stand up to the Boss, had the guts to recommend a franchise-altering cultural change, and had the conviction to challenge his managers. He's also had to take hardline approaches with players, and no one example of this is more memorable than his free-agent negotiations with Derek Jeter.

In February of 2001, Jeter, coming off his fourth World Series championship as the starting shortstop for the Yankees, agreed to a contract extension of $189 million over the next ten seasons. Had Jeter waited to reach free agency, he surely could have made more money on the open market, but at the time, staying a Yankee was his priority, as was winning his fifth World Series.[19]

In 2010, primed to reach free agency for the first time in his career, Jeter had long assumed the money he left on the table in 2001 would be made up in good faith during his next negotiations. He had seen the front office give away millions in cash to teammates over the years,[20] as if dollars were dirt. Jeter was the captain of the Yankees, he helped them win five World Series championships, and he was well on his way to a Hall of Fame career. But a couple of factors worked against him during this round of negotiations: George Steinbrenner—one of Jeter's biggest allies—had passed away during the 2010 season. In addition, Jeter's on-field performance that season had produced many career lows and gave the Yankees' executives pause—at age thirty-six, would Jeter ever be as impactful or valuable as he had been for them to that point? It was a fair question for both parties to ponder.

---

[19] Jeter later got his fifth title—although he did have to wait eight seasons for it.
[20] Some of whom included Mike Mussina, Jason Giambi, and his counterpart on the left side of the infield, Alex Rodriguez.

Jeter wanted top money, and Cashman wanted to pay him closer to what the baseball market perceived as fair value. Cashman offered Jeter a three-year contract for $51 million. Jeter was shocked and appalled at what he felt was a low-ball offer from his employer. The truth was—and Cashman was correct in this assessment—that no team in baseball would offer a thirty-six-year-old shortstop, coming off one of his worst seasons, anything close to the type of money the Yankees had. Good faith *was* being rewarded by the Yankees, even if Jeter refused to see it as such.

With Jeter unwilling to budge on his expectations, Cashman dug in and did what all great executives need to do in a tense situation between a franchise player and the employer: He told Jeter and his agent, Casey Close, to go out in the open market and shop for a better deal.

This move was a risk on Cashman's part. If there was a club daring enough to see Derek Jeter in any uniform but the Yankee pinstripes, then the two parties could have been headed for a messy divorce. But Close and his client shopped around, and they gloomily returned to the Yankees' executives with the discovery that no team was desperate enough to go above Cashman's offer.

Even so, Cashman held to his initial bid; he didn't offer Jeter more money out of pity or even out of desperation, as the negotiation began to messily play out in the public. Either Jeter took the money, or the shortstop would have to walk away from the Yankees.

Ultimately, Jeter decided to take the deal and re-sign. In the end, the shortstop would play his remaining four seasons with the Yankees, finishing as the franchise's all-time leader in hits (3,465) and games played (2,747).

Cashman had preserved a key organizational relationship and managed it through the rocky moments of the negotiation. In doing so, he had raised his profile as one of the game's top executives, and in one of the first major moments for the Yankees since the death of George Steinbrenner, he'd shown that he had the marbles to handle major responsibilities as a leader.

Supplementing Internal Development with Outside Reinforcements

Cashman's primary responsibility is to make the Yankees good enough to win a championship each season. The GM says of his role, "My job is to get as much talent as I can so we take a shot at the title. If I do my job well, we'll get multiple shots."

Having been in the organization long before taking over as GM in 1998, Cashman is fully cognizant of the poor player-development practices of Yankees past, and he knows that gutting the team at the lower ranks for major-league-ready talent can have long-term effects that will be more debilitating than rewarding. George Steinbrenner had run them into the ground during the 1980s doing just that. Thus, he's become the type of executive who tries to find *value* for every player and every position.

There is rarely a day when Cashman doesn't need to make a baseball-related decision. These decisions all have different contexts, with short-term impact and sometimes long-term consequences.

Cashman finds himself on the winning side more often than not, such as trading for David Justice in 2000—who won the ALCS MVP that year and helped the Yankees win the Subway Series versus the crosstown-rival Mets.[21]

During the 1998 trade deadline, Cashman found himself fending off executives for a tall left-handed pitcher on the Seattle Mariners named Randy Johnson. Here was the scenario: Cashman refused to give up the group of Yankees players and prospects the Mariners were asking for, but felt that if another team in the AL got Johnson, he would have lost his job as GM before he ever got comfortable. Cashman didn't want to deplete the Yankees' depth for only one player—albeit a game-changing pitcher—but that was of little worry to Steinbrenner, who would never have let Cashman live it down if

---

[21] The Subway Series refers to the 2000 World Series between the New York Yankees and the New York Mets.

Johnson was traded within the league and haunted the Yankees in the playoffs.

Fortunately for Cashman, the Houston Astros traded for Johnson,[22] and the GM had accomplished what he set out to do. The power-lefty was in another league and far away from the Yankees. The only worry Cashman had was if the Astros and Yankees matched up in the World Series. What if Johnson dominated the Yankees, and the Astros won the World Series? What would Steinbrenner say then?

That doomsday scenario, of course, did not happen. At least not in 1998. But remember those long-term consequences to *all* decisions?

Three seasons later, Cashman's worst nightmare became a reality. Johnson, now a member of the Arizona Diamondbacks, dominated the Yankees in two starts during the 2001 World Series. He then pitched out of the bullpen during Game 7 as Arizona came back to defeat the Yankees in the desert, effectively ending the dynasty. The cherry on top: Johnson was named co-MVP of the series.

You can't predict baseball, Suzyn.[23]

A more recent loss on Cashman's permanent record came as a result of his inability to persuade the new boss to bring in reinforcements. Cashman petitioned hard with ownership for the green light to acquire pitcher Justin Verlander in August of 2017. But Hal Steinbrenner vetoed adding to the payroll,[24] which allowed the Houston Astros to pounce on the pitcher. Verlander, thrust into the middle of a pennant race, pitched masterfully for the remainder of the 2017 regular season. Then in the playoffs, he added salt to the wound by throwing a classic performance in a 7–1 ALCS Game 6 win, setting the Astros up to win the series versus the Yankees in seven games.

---

[22] At that point, the Astros were still a member of the National League.

[23] This is a phrase made famous by Suzyn Waldman's radio sidekick, John Sterling.

[24] Verlander was scheduled to make more than $28 million annually over the next four seasons, through 2021.

Although he doesn't always win, Cashman is often able to fend off other teams and acquire the asset. During the 2018–19 off-season, DJ LeMahieu was being looked at by multiple teams, among them the Yankees and division-rival Tampa Bay Rays. Cashman convinced LeMahieu to come to New York, even though at the time it seemed the former All-Star for the Colorado Rockies would be used as a "super-utility" player.[25] But when injuries ravaged the Yankees' roster in early 2019, LeMahieu saw his playing time increase immensely, and he produced an MVP-caliber regular season for the ball club—finishing fourth in that season's voting.

Cashman has missed before, especially in terms of his ability to acquire quality starting pitching via trade or free agency—save for the 2019 off-season signing of ace pitcher, Gerrit Cole. Cashman will miss again in the future. But more often than not, he's able to make calculated and data-driven decisions that help him acquire the very exact player the team needs, even if it doesn't look anything like what the old regime would have done.

It's called *fiscal responsibility*; the modern Yankees try not to spend money just to make an impression or react to another team's bold move (Google "Kei Igawa's stats" for more on that disastrous strategy). If Cashman doesn't feel a player fits the Yankees' mold, then he won't pursue them. The fit matters most—it's as simple as that.

What do the kids say these days about their GM of more than twenty seasons?

In Cash We Trust.

By challenging conventional wisdom in New York, Cashman has found innovative ways to significantly improve the organization. His formula for success is simple: He invests in structure, scouting, playing development, and analytics. He no longer spends gobs of dough on one or more players in free agency, just to spend it. Cashman sinks his greatest resource, *money*, into assets that matter

---

[25] Meaning he was a versatile player and could play anywhere in the infield.

most, like talent, character, and the continuous supply chain that will produce top-line Yankee prospects.

George Steinbrenner chose to spend his money on proven commodities that came without a long shelf life. Cashman prefers the new methodology, which he feels to be more thorough and realistic for *efficient sustainable success*. Because that's really what the job is about.

The purpose is to win, *not* burn the team into the ground for one championship. Brian Cashman understands this approach better than anyone who worked in the front office during the Steinbrenner era.

Hal Steinbrenner: A Forward Way of Doing Business

"I hold on to competent people so that they can make decisions that don't involve me."

These are words spoken by the Yankees' current principal owner, managing general partner, and co-chairman, Hal Steinbrenner. The message by the youngest son of George Steinbrenner gives insight into an individual who is measured in his demeanor and appearance. Hal Steinbrenner doesn't have his dad's intense mood swings, and his acumen for what is needed in today's baseball world could not be better suited to align with Brian Cashman's vision for the present-day Yankees.

It's well known within the Yankee Universe that Steinbrenner did *not* ask for the job as the patriarch of the franchise. But when his father's health began to decline in the mid-2000s, Steinbrenner's mother, Joan, and his siblings insisted he was the rightful heir to the greatest franchise in sports.

Hal Steinbrenner took over the day-to-day operations from his father permanently in 2008. His outlook was to guide the Yankees toward a future that was just as exciting as the past eras, but was also more *cost-effective* than his father's version. Although his long-term vision was conceptually different from his father's, Steinbrenner didn't break stride from the Boss overnight.

During the 2008–09 off-season, the Yankees committed $423.5 million to sign three players to long-term deals, bolstering a weak pitching staff with CC Sabathia and AJ Burnett and adding a young, elite hitter to their lineup, switch-hitting first baseman Mark Teixeira. The spending spree resulted in the organization's twenty-seventh World Series championship in 2009.

After the 2009 season, the Yankees were still winning—although they didn't win another title—and were printing big money at the ballpark gates. But in 2012 the roster again began to show cracks, and it was becoming apparent that age was catching up to some of the veteran stars.

Jorge Posada retired after the 2011 season, Mariano Rivera was lost for the season in May 2012 with a knee injury, and then Derek Jeter broke his ankle during the 2012 season's Game 1 loss of the ALCS.

In the 2013 season injuries continued to pile up, as Jeter missed significant time during his ankle-injury recovery, and Alex Rodriguez and Teixeira, among others, missed time during the season due to various injuries. Though they stayed in the hunt through the first 157 regular-season games, the Yankees were eventually eliminated from postseason contention for the first time since 2008 and only the second time since the strike-shortened 1994 season.

The bottom was falling out, and to make matters worse, the hated Red Sox won their third World Series title in ten seasons. The Yankees' payroll sat well above the luxury tax threshold (which acts as a soft salary cap in baseball and penalizes teams that spend above the number)—which meant they were paying more than $1 million each season to other franchises—and because of the crippling injuries, they had become unwatchable.

During the 2013–14 off-season, Hal Steinbrenner approved one more desperate attempt to stay on par with past practices. Andy Pettitte and Rivera had retired after the 2013 campaign, and

Rodriguez was suspended for the entire 2014 season in connection with the Biogenesis scandal.[26]

Question marks were all over the now-elusive identity of the team. So, the Yankees decided to throw money at the problem. First, Japanese pitching ace Masahiro Tanaka got a seven-year, $155 million contract, and then the Yankees lured center fielder Jacoby Ellsbury away from archrival Boston for seven years, $153 million.[27] Brian McCann was given a five-year, $85 million contract, and after the team added Carlos Beltrán for three years at $45 million, the Yankees had committed close to $500 million to four players that off-season.

The results of that spending spree were not quite the same as they were during the 2008–09 off-season. The Yankees did not win a World Series, they continued to get older, and Brian Cashman's vision for a more cost-controlled future was becoming a more likely scenario the longer the Yankees hung around as, at best, an average team. It's not that Hal Steinbrenner wasn't initially on board with the plan to go rogue, but breaking stride from family practices is challenging, as if running a business isn't demanding enough.

Since those lean years in Yankees history, Steinbrenner and Cashman have developed a working relationship that centers around a Joe Torre classic: *Trust*. Building a trust-bond with Cashman has allowed Steinbrenner to run the franchise as he sees fit *and* stay true to the values that set him apart from the Boss.

To be absolutely clear, Hal Steinbrenner does have the final say in all decisions, but he says, "Ninety percent of what Cash wants gets done because I trust him and his people. They know a lot more about this stuff than I do."

Built within the trust between Steinbrenner and Cashman is the belief that financial decisions affect the capability of the team in a way that George Steinbrenner never could see. Hal Steinbrenner

---

[26] The scandal accused several major league players of using performance-enhancing drugs from the clinic Biogenesis of America.
[27] During the final three seasons of Ellsbury's contract (2018–2020), the Yankees paid him a boatload of money to play in exactly ZERO games.

admits that his father was "a micromanager" as a leader, and that his ruthless desire to always win clouded his vision for how to run a sustainable organization.

"Now we struggled for years," Steinbrenner began explaining, "because our development system was lacking and we had nobody to come up and help out. My dad tended, as you know, to trade away good young people to win now, now, now, now.

"I can't tell you how many times over the last five years, teams asked us for [Aaron] Judge and [Gary] Sánchez and [Luis] Severino and others, and year after year we refused. So now here we are, with all these young stars that we can promote to our fans on social media and a system where everybody still wants our minor leaguers now that these guys have come up. I don't take credit for much, but I *will* take credit for that, and Cash was right on board with me."

In overcoming resistance to the change in ownership, it will be important to highlight what will stay the same—the Yankees' mandate to win. Aspiring to change is more appealing when it's paired with visions of continuity. The Yankees' culture and processes might evolve, but their identity will remain intact.

The future of the New York Yankees lies in better money-management processes, a more patient approach toward player development, and a firm belief that a *Culture of Excellence* is *the* roadmap toward sustainability and success. If the disciples of George Steinbrenner won't get on board with those ideas, then too bad—they can find the closest exit and leave. Hal Steinbrenner and his front office aren't drunk on the exceptionalism of Yankees past, and they won't be constrained by the phrase "What would George have done?"

The ability of Hal Steinbrenner to break away from his father's idealism and innovate based on his own values *will* be the single biggest contributor toward the sustained success of the Yankees for years to come.

Summary of the *Evil Empire Architects*

The dynamic between Brian Cashman and Hal Steinbrenner is unlike any relationship that George Steinbrenner had with a front-office executive. Cashman and George Steinbrenner were able to build a coexisting relationship, but the Boss always had the final say on baseball-related matters. Now there is more of a mutual understanding and trust built between Hal Steinbrenner and Cashman, with the biggest difference being that the two work *with* one another, and not *for* one another.

Without Cashman doing the heavy lifting toward the end of the George Steinbrenner era, there's a chance that the current model of the Yankees' excellence wouldn't exist. Cashman's efforts highlight the need to be *tough-skinned, innovative, and patient.*

Hal Steinbrenner has displayed a readiness to exercise the latter two traits, while also showing a willingness to be fiscally responsible without giving up on the company mandate to compete for championships. This allows Cashman to have the full toolbox at his disposal when assembling a roster and building an organization that many want to replicate, but few have the resources or the moxie to make a reality.

KEY POINTS: LEADERSHIP

Leadership is not a burden, but effective leadership is difficult to achieve. There is a common perception that anyone can be a leader, but until a person assumes the responsibilities of managing people, they often don't realize what they are actually being held accountable for.

If there is one focal point to take away from this pillar, it is *patience*. Many of the leaders featured here didn't find "excellence" right away, and they endured through many of the same trials and tribulations that most individuals experience in life. But these people had the humility and self-awareness to learn from their mistakes, and they were able to accomplish amazing feats in arguably one of the most difficult settings imaginable. If they aren't models for success, then who is?

Many additional leadership attributes were highlighted in this pillar:

- *Being a pioneer*
- *Having a ruthless desire to succeed*
- *Learning to trust*
- *Bringing stability*
- *Building and managing relationships*
- *Being innovative*
- *Having self-awareness*
- *Achieving fiscal responsibility*

These aren't the *only* leadership qualities an individual can possess, but what great benchmarks they are.

The stories of George Steinbrenner, Joe Torre, Joe Girardi, Aaron Boone, Brian Cashman, and Hal Steinbrenner are all unique—and they are specific to the individual and the time period in which they led or are leading. Each person understood where their strengths could contribute to success, and most times, they were able to supplement their weaknesses by asking for help from others. Their anecdotes serve as the leading foundation (pun intended) for the Yankees' *Culture of Excellence*, and they can provide you with the framework to build your own.

PILLAR TWO

CULTURE—PEOPLE AND COMMUNITY

Culture *(noun)* - the set of shared attitudes, values, goals, and practices that characterizes an institution or organization

"If a guy wasn't doing his job or dogging it a little bit, we could get on that guy face-to-face. The guys were ready to play most of the time, but if it needed to be done—the few times—nobody had a problem on this team going to somebody else and telling them, 'Let's go. You need to do this and that.' And that player would understand."

- Tino Martinez

Chapter Four

Culture

I t's quite possible that culture is an even bigger buzzword than leadership. In sports, corporate, retail, hospitality … you name it—culture is the word that industry leaders are most concerned with. If the "culture" isn't there, then they can't get anyone to work for them. But as with leaders, it's very easy for people to spot a phony environment. Having core values listed on a sign in an office or on a company website doesn't constitute what culture truly encompasses, because the culture isn't about words. It's about people and experiences.

The clubhouse and organizational culture of the New York Yankees, like Rome, wasn't built in a day. Seeds had to be planted by early pioneers, such as former general manager Gene Michael and manager Buck Showalter, and they were watered to grow and flourish during the Joe Torre era. Even during the Joe Girardi era, the roots of those seeds continued to grow larger to produce today's franchise, which is one of the best examples of a robust culture in all of sports— and some would argue, even in the business world.

How does one build the type of culture the Yankees have achieved? It starts with expectations. The Yankees *expect* to win each season, and even when they don't, they usually do all they can to give the team the resources it needs to compete. As a result, the players continue to grind until they are officially eliminated from contention.

Chad Green, an integral pitcher in the vaunted Yankees' bullpen, drives home the confidence that the organization exudes. "With the Yankees, winning is just kind of expected," says the Yankees reliever. "I came up with the [Detroit] Tigers and it's just different. Maybe it's more expected here in the minor leagues than other places.

"There's a reason the Yankees have won twenty-seven world championships. It's not something that's discussed, but I guess you just kind of know. They preach winning in the minors so when it gets up here, it gets more natural because it's expected up here. I think it all starts in the minors with the personnel and staff they have there."

Brian Cashman empowers his minor league chain to demonstrate the winning culture at every level and with all of its players. The organization has invested money into sports science, analytics, and the psychosocial training of its young prospects—an expenditure that pays dividends once a player reaches the big leagues. The Baby Bombers are *prepared* once they reach the big leagues.

The Yankees have minor league instructors and coaches that are hardworking and positive. In other organizations, those people are jaded ex-major leaguers who perpetuate a culture of complaining that nothing is ever as good as it can be. These types of people never got their "big break" and want other players to suffer as they did, even if their job is supposed to be helping them develop. That type of thought process doesn't exist in Yankee Universe; such behavior is strictly prohibited.

Suzyn Waldman, one half of the Yankees' play-by-play radio voice with sidekick John Sterling, echoes Green's earlier assessment of the Yankees' organizational culture. "These players have all grown up where winning is the only important thing," she starts. "The things that they say, it's more than they're having fun. They've got an idea of what it takes to be a Yankee and succeed here."

What does it take to be a Yankee and succeed in New York, Suzyn?

It takes talent, a strong mental aptitude, and a grasping of the historic tradition of the Yankees. The Yankees' Hall of Famer, Mariano Rivera, once said, "The pinstripes are heavy in New York." Another

Yankees' Hall of Famer, Reggie Jackson, added, "When you first come here, I think it takes time for some of the younger people to understand the Yankee way.

"The whole organization has a feeling about continuing—and I say this with respect—the way the old guard wanted it. The way the sheriff [George Steinbrenner] wanted it is how we want to continue to do things."

As the game of baseball trends toward younger players each season, there is a premium being placed on having the team's prospects understand and embrace the "Yankee way." Playing for the Yankees is, for most people, the opportunity of a lifetime. If a player can work through the pressures and demands, more often than not they'll be rewarded with a true opportunity to compete on the game's biggest stage each October during the playoffs.

A Lesson in Organizational Dysfunction

Corporate exceptionalism is absurd. A lot of teams in the sports world get drunk off their exceptionalism, which has an impact that can damage a franchise for years.

The Yankees don't operate that way … anymore. Remember the Bronx Zoo? Yeah, it's actually not that long ago. But the Yankees of the twenty-first century operate less like a zoo and more like a university research program. They are constantly on the hunt, gathering new data and information, while creating an inclusive culture for all the players to participate in.

Brian Cashman says of the current regime, "We go out of our way to eradicate any arrogance and, by doing so, fill the void with a thirst for knowledge and being open-minded."

Organizational dysfunction has also happened before at places that are now known for more good than bad. Take, for example, Apple Inc., where Steve Jobs was forced out of the company in 1985 because of his obsession with control;[28] there was a power struggle between

---

[28] Jobs was a co-founder of the tech giant.

him and his business partner and friend, Steve Wozniak. But Jobs further compounded his bad standing when he also wouldn't let talented employees come up with innovative ideas and wound up firing the majority of them before they could ever make significant contributions to the company.

During his time away from Apple over the next decade, Jobs was able to revamp his professional career. When he returned to Apple in 1997, it marked the beginning of an unprecedented tech boom for the company. Jobs received much of the credit for leading Apple into the new millennium and setting it up to be the largest giant of them all, but his later-life success would have been impossible to achieve had he not learned from his past failure and made a significant change in his leadership style.

The Yankees used to suffer mightily due to instability and drama. George Steinbrenner would hire Billy Martin. Then fire him. Then rehire him. Then fire Martin again.

During the darker years, Steinbrenner liked to pick fights with his most visible assets as a way to remind them that he was the Boss. His biographer, Bill Madden, wrote of the owner, "If there was one pattern in Steinbrenner's motivational style, it was to pick on the biggest star on the team, usually not long after they'd signed long-term contracts."

Steinbrenner was also a victim of listening to too much outside noise, usually because he wanted to be well received. He would hear fans turning on him, panic, make bad trades, and the Yankees' on-field struggles would only worsen. Inadvertently or not, Steinbrenner wanted to control everything so badly that he sucked the life out of the Yankees, decimating them to resemble the likes of the awful clubs from the late 1960s.

There was little "winning" in the Boss's world during the period 1979-1995, and the Yankees reflected that, appearing in only one World Series (which they lost) and three additional playoff series.

Like Steve Jobs, George Steinbrenner eventually evolved as a leader during a forced time away, and ultimately each organization came out on the other side a more reputable company with more capable leadership.

Emerging Leaders

Change is inevitable each baseball season. New players sign with a team, others retire, some even get demoted. But there is a certain order to the ranks of players in a baseball clubhouse.

In baseball's past, experienced veterans were much less welcoming of young players who threatened their place on the roster. Veteran ballplayers once felt compelled to haze a rookie and make clear the power structure that existed.

What good does it do to make a young player—or any person coming in, for that matter—feel unwelcome? Isn't the point for the new people to immediately contribute? How are they expected to produce if they are being victimized?

Even the Yankees had players who used to exhibit this poor behavior toward teammates. When a young Bernie Williams first came to New York in 1991, he was referred to as "Bambi," because he was perceived by some as "soft." Mel Hall, then a Yankee outfielder who moonlighted as the clubhouse bully, called Williams "Zero" and mocked him at every turn, determined to break the center fielder's spirit.

That type of behavior is no longer accepted across much of baseball, especially within the Yankees' clubhouse. Former pitcher CC Sabathia—a victim of hazing and detrimental treatment as a rookie with the Cleveland Indians—was the chief enforcer of that policy. But to learn how to be an influencer like Sabathia—now a special advisor to the Yankees—one must know more about his story.

Sabathia's journey to becoming a clubhouse leader was, at one point, just as unlikely as it would have been for George Steinbrenner to keep a manager longer than two seasons. A man who wears his feelings on his sleeve and enjoys the game of baseball more than most, Sabathia began experiencing personal and professional battles beginning in 2013.

The Yankees' ace pitcher struggled in 2013, compiling a 4.78 earned run average before he was shut down for the rest of the season with a hamstring injury. The rehab that Sabathia underwent to recover from the most severe injury of his career began to pull at his ability to control and restrain himself, especially when it came to one of his favorite vices: alcohol.

As the injury rehab became harder and his struggles continued, Sabathia found himself boozing harder. It was reported during this time that he was often capable of wiping out entire mini-fridges of alcohol during road trips, and in 2015, he was caught on camera in Toronto getting into a verbal altercation with a patron outside a bar. Sabathia has since said that trying to hide his drinking actually became more exhausting than getting drunk.

While his career and life spiraled out of control, his wife, Amber, urged her husband to seek treatment for his alcohol abuse. Finally, after two long and trying seasons, Sabathia checked himself into rehab on the last day of the 2015 season. Once an indispensable player to the team's championship dreams, Sabathia was now absent from the Yankees' Wild Card playoff game—a home contest they lost 3-0 to the Houston Astros.

Sabathia was at a crossroads in his career and in his life and needed to make dramatic changes if he were to survive. Starting with alcohol rehab, Sabathia transformed. As of this writing, he's been sober for over four years, and he pitched well enough through his initial Yankees contract to get offered one-year extensions in both 2018 and 2019 before retiring following the 2019 season.

His ability to contribute on the field was important, but Sabathia's skill as a leader off the field also weighed heavily in the organization's decision to continue bringing him back into the fold. That Sabathia eventually grew into being able to handle the reins of a clubhouse leader is of little surprise. His former manager, Joe Girardi, says of the pitcher, "He's a better person than he is a player. He's great to have in the clubhouse."

When the Yankees were recruiting Sabathia after the 2008 season, the pitcher was most interested in the clubhouse culture. He'd heard the rumors of a strained superstar relationship between Derek Jeter and Alex Rodriguez, as well as an overall splintering of the culture that had completely torn down the armor from the dynasty years.

Brian Cashman recalled the meeting with Sabathia, saying, "CC's main concern was our clubhouse and how people got along. We had a reputation for not being together. We had a reputation of fighting each other, and that was a big concern there.

"I told him the truth," Cashman continued. "Yeah, we are broken. One reason we're committing to you is you're a team builder. We need somebody that brings us all together."

Sabathia was in the first wave of players to enter into the refocused efforts Cashman was implementing to replicate the cultural likeness of the dynasty teams. There wasn't an immediate need in 2009 for all that Sabathia could offer, walking into a club with established leaders and veterans. However, as the seasons passed and players moved on, it was Sabathia who stood as perhaps the biggest influence on a culture which, during his time in New York, became younger and more inexperienced than in prior years.

Sabathia wanted players to come up or arrive in New York and have the ability to produce. It was a common sight over the years to see young prospects hang around the elder statesman's locker and listen to him talk about baseball and life.

While he's off enjoying retirement, Sabathia will hand the reins to another Yankee(s)—most likely, Brett Gardner and/or Aaron Judge—who will uphold the culture code. Sabathia faced adversity due to injuries and alcoholism, but he bounced back and provided invaluable leadership during his career in New York. His story beautifully highlights that even great leaders can go through difficult times, but they have the opportunity to return to a position of influence.

Players on the Yankees appreciate the competition that the game of baseball provides. Competition can cause people to tense up or leave a situation altogether—but for the Yankees it serves a useful purpose: strengthening the team. It can be very motivating to have someone always coming to win a job, whether they are at the major league level or lingering in the minors.

Brett Gardner, the Yankees' longest-tenured player and another clubhouse leader, describes his early relationship with Johnny Damon, a major league veteran with championship pedigree: "He's one of the guys that really helped kind of take me under his wing and feel comfortable. And at the end of the day, I was trying to take Johnny's job from him as a young guy."

Johnny Damon had the confidence in himself to be a mentor and knew that an improved and comfortable Gardner would be of more value to the Yankees than one who was suppressed and tormented. As a result, Damon and Gardner both ended up contributing in roles that helped the Yankees win the World Series in 2009.

Beginning in 2017, the Yankees' crowded outfield, as well as Gardner's declining skills and production, has the situation repeating itself. Clint Frazier is one of many within the organization vying for routine playing time in the outfield. What does Brett think of the contest?

"I've got to respect his work ethic and the way he goes about his business," Gardner stated. "And I'm sure that he does the same to me. It's my job to be as good as I can be and try to keep him from taking my job."

Healthy competition and uplifting others—these are key ingredients to success.

It Feels Like Home

The clubhouse is where a team spends the majority of their time during a season, both at home and while on the road. Cultural improvements can be as much about tangible attributes as they are about attitudes and behaviors of people. If the physical area doesn't have a good feel to it, it can be very difficult to relax and be comfortable.

The construction of the current Yankees' clubhouse began during the Buck Showalter era, when the manager decided to install a family room for the players' young kids. Next came an improvement to the weight room. Over the years, the Yankees' clubhouse transformed to become first-rate, especially when the franchise moved across the street into the new Yankee Stadium.

The Yankees' current place is thirty thousand square feet, over twice the space of the one in the original stadium. It features a weight room, training room, video room, and lounge area. There is also a physical therapy room that includes a hydrotherapy pool with an underwater treadmill. And, of course, there is the highly coveted indoor batting cage, which is good for use at any time of day or at any point in a game.

There is also strategic planning that goes into locker assignments within a clubhouse. Back when a young Derek Jeter came to the Bronx, he found his locker next to that of Don Mattingly. The Yankees did this so that one captain could pass his knowledge to a player the Yankees hoped would one day take over the responsibility as a leader.

In a future clubhouse, the team decided to place Gleyber Torres and Didi Gregorius next to each other when Torres, the highly touted rookie, was called up to the big leagues in April of 2018. As one of the *de facto* leaders of the Yankees, it made sense to give Torres a spot next to someone who carried Gregorius's cool attitude, as well as his professionalism.

Other cultural ventures expand outside of the clubhouse. Joe Girardi instituted a "Family Day" during his tenure as manager, time that was filled with family, food, face painting, and different play stations for kids spread across the field at Yankee Stadium. Aaron Boone continues that tradition with his current squad.

During Girardi's managerial stint, he also brought individuals from outside the organization into the clubhouse to share their experiences and expertise: people like University of Alabama head football coach, Nick Saban, and United States Olympian sprinter, Michael Johnson. It may not seem like professional athletes need extra motivation to assist them in performing, but over the course of a long season, a fresh voice and an influential person can jolt a team or help it refocus.

Ultimately, a team is like a second family. Why not try to make it feel as much like home as possible? It's easy to tell when a clubhouse feels close and tight-knit. When players hang around longer than they need to *and* also make plans to do extracurriculars together when they leave the ballpark … that's the magic all teams strive for.

Blending Unique Personalities

Individualism is an enormous part of the identity of millennials. The tech giant Google has a popular "80/20" company policy that grants (and encourages) employees to spend 20 percent of their working time on creative side projects of their choice.

By empowering their employees with the ownership to do work that is creative, in addition to the responsibilities they are paid for, Google has seen innovative ideas come to the company that may not have otherwise been discovered. They've also had workers create products and services so large that they ended up venturing off on their own. Google's giving its employees creative freedom has built a culture of happy, hardworking, and innovative individuals, and it's resulted in the company becoming not only a leader in its industry, but globally as well.

The Yankees have employed their share of creative personalities, and while the wave of imaginative and artistic players is hardly new to the team or the sport, it is more prevalent now than at any point before.

Back during the Yankees' dynasty of the 1990s, players like Paul O'Neill and Bernie Williams used music as an outlet from the day-today grind of the long baseball season.[29] Williams, who has produced two major albums, released his first record, *The Journey Within*, in 2003 while he was still a member of the Yankees.

Derek Jeter hosted an episode of the television comedy *Saturday Night Live* in 2001—although to be fair, he appeared on the show *after* the season was over. As a player, Joe Girardi was an active member of the negotiation committee for the Major League Baseball Players Association (MLBPA)—their union representation in the sport.

In recent years, baseball has encouraged players to show more of their personality, and that has resulted in an array of creative schticks by individuals and teams. Didi Gregorius, who was arguably the Yankees' funniest player during his time in New York, was author of emoji-filled victory tweets that highlighted outstanding players and usually began with #StartSpreadingTheNews,[30] and ended with "WHAT A GAME!!!"

Fans had fun trying to determine which players were what emoji (seriously, there are lists out on the internet), and the Yankees' official Twitter account always made sure to highlight their star shortstop with a retweet and his own emoji,[31] because Gregorius, the ultimate team player, never wanted the celebration to be about him (even if it was warranted).

Gregorius is also an avid photographer and artist, and during his rehab from Tommy John Surgery between the 2018 off-season and the beginning of the 2019 season,[32] he created his first digital piece of art animation. It depicted his first-inning, three-run home run in the

---

[29] O'Neill banged on the drums and Williams is a classically trained guitarist.

[30] A reference to singer Frank Sinatra's "Theme from *New York, New York*" that plays at the conclusion of every Yankee home game.

[31] Emojis are defined as any of various small images, symbols, or icons used in text fields in electronic communication (such as text messages, email, and social media) to express the emotional attitude of the writer, convey information succinctly, communicate a message playfully without using words, etc.

[32] According to Johns Hopkins Medicine, Tommy John Surgery, more formally known as ulnar collateral ligament (UCL) reconstruction, is used to repair a torn ulnar collateral ligament inside the elbow.

2017 Wild Card Game that set Yankee Stadium fans into pandemonium.

Whether he's painting, tweeting, smashing home runs, or holding up emoji sticks on the dugout steps, Didi Gregorius is the quintessential person to highlight the millennial innovativeness.

But he's not the only one to get into the entertainment.

In 2017, former Yankees Todd Frazier and Ronald Torreyes added to the fun already provided by Gregorius. First, Frazier authored the "thumbs down" signal. The backstory here started on September 11, 2017, during a game at Citi Field versus the Tampa Bay Rays. The Rays had to move their home games to Queens, New York, due to Hurricane Irma, and during the broadcast, YES Network cameras found a Mets fan in the stands giving Frazier a thumbs down for a home run the third baseman had just hit.[33]

Someone showed Frazier the clip on social media, and he decided to have fun with it. Frazier first gave the signal to teammates two days later as a way to celebrate a base hit. After that, the thumbs down spread throughout the Yankees and was a great rallying cry during the Baby Bomber run of 2017.

Adding to the amusement was a production created by Torreyes (nicknamed "Toe") that would be dubbed "The Toe-night Show." The "show," which occurred inside the Yankees' dugout, featured Gregorius as the primary interviewer and Torreyes as the cameraman.[34] "The Toe-night Show" became a sensation on social media and with Yankees fans, and although it was ultimately even more short-lived than the thumbs down, both creative outlets let the 2017 Yankees express themselves in unique ways on the field and in competition.

In another medium, R2C2 is a collaborative podcasting effort put together by CC Sabathia and the Yankees' broadcaster and analyst,

---

[33] The YES Network ("YES" stands for "Yankees Entertainment and Sports Network") is the official television station of the New York Yankees. The fan was later identified as Gary Dunaier.

[34] Gregorius used an upside-down paper cup as a microphone. Torreyes used a bin that held sunflower seeds as a camera.

Ryan Ruocco. Sabathia and Ruocco are honest and open about all topics they chat about, which include but aren't limited to music, culture, and of course, sports. Guests, such as Mark Cuban, Sue Bird, and a wide array of major league players—current and former—have graced the show for personal interviews not heard too widely within the scope of big-league baseball.

Sabathia and Ruocco also have plenty of Yankees players on the show, and fans get a unique experience from listening to their favorite players while learning more about their background or what drives them to be successful.

One can tell from the listening experience that it's enjoyable for the guests and for Sabathia and Ruocco—the latter of whom can often be heard laughing hysterically at a story from a guest, or at the expense of one another. R2C2 is both fresh in its originality and real in its content, which makes it a must-listen-to podcast.

Back on the field in 2019, there were plenty of fun moments that saw Yankees players expressing themselves in ways the sport wasn't so accustomed to. Early in the season, they introduced the Player of the Game (or Championship) belt, blue leather with the interlocking "NY" in gold, which was passed around after each victory to the player who had earned the distinctive right and honor. Players had fun with the ritual, often posing for a postgame picture with the belt on, and then proudly displaying the belt in their locker until it was passed to the next deserving soul.

In addition to the belt, one of the funnier displays of creativity in 2019 came at the expense of Edwin Encarnación. Prior to joining the Yankees early in the 2019 season, Encarnación had established a home run ritual of rounding the bases with his right elbow raised at ninety degrees. Thus, Encarnación earned the nickname "Parrot," as one could imagine the bird perched atop Encarnación's arm while trotting toward home plate.

The Yankees' players took the moniker a step further when they introduced a stuffed animal that they gave to Encarnación each time he returned to the dugout after hitting another homer. While major league rules prohibit the stuffed parrot from entering the playing field, the club still found different ways to have fun with the bird—like the time they had Encarnación pose for a picture on a flight in which the parrot is buckled into the next seat.

The content that players and teams can create and are eager to participate in will only increase in the years ahead. Whether it's a result of the "savages in the box" Aaron Boone ejection meltdown, #LetBrettBang, or a more personal interest toward having a creative outlet, imaginative renderings will continue to be a part of the culture of the Yankees and of baseball.

Frailty of Human Life

Ballplayers are, of course, humans. Beneath the layers of entertainment, money, and competition they're *people* who go through the same rollercoaster of life as everyone else. While athletes may be held to a higher performance standard than an average worker, they still have the same wants, needs, and desires as any warm-blooded mammal.

In 1996, Joe Torre unexpectedly lost a brother to a massive heart attack. Another brother underwent a heart transplant during the World Series that same year, and prior to the start of the 1999 season Torre received more hard news: He had been diagnosed with prostate cancer and needed surgery to stop it from spreading.

Torre would have a successful surgery and return to manage the Yankees in 1999 and beyond. Because of his upbringing and personal experience, Torre would become a *de facto* emotional leader during his time as manager.

In 1999, Yankees' third baseman Scott Brosius's father had been diagnosed with colon cancer. As his father's condition worsened throughout the season, Brosius would continually ask Torre for permission to go home to Oregon. Torre always said yes, understanding that if Brosius's mind was elsewhere it wasn't helpful for him to be around.

People shouldn't be prevented from seeking emotional peace.

Brosius's father passed from cancer in mid-September of 1999, and just as the Yankees were gearing to wrap up another championship that October, Paul O'Neill got an early morning call informing him that his father, who had been suffering from heart disease, had also passed. O'Neill, known affectionately as "The Warrior," and an emotional leader, took his customary spot in right field and controlled his emotions until the final out of Game 4, a Yankees' World Series victory. He then openly wept on the field during the championship celebration, and was consoled by none other than Torre.

All of the personal struggles the 1999 Yankees endured came on the heels of the stunning diagnosis given in the fall of 1998 to another emotional leader, slugger Darryl Strawberry, who also had colon cancer. Strawberry's fight against cancer came as New York was preparing for Game 3 of the American League Division Series versus the Texas Rangers. When Torre addressed the club prior to working out, the manager's voice cracked and players started to sob. The situation rocked the Yankees, but they were able to band together and win the World Series while proudly displaying a white "39"— Strawberry's number with the team—on the back of their hats, symbolizing their collective thoughts and prayers for their teammate.

Two seasons earlier, in May of 1996, Strawberry's teammate David Cone found himself in a dicey situation. Cone had an aneurysm in his pitching arm that required immediate surgery and put the rest of his season in doubt. Cone's year was likely over, and his prognosis, although not considered life-threatening, was a major shakeup to the pitcher and the Yankees' personnel.

Cone recovered remarkably fast and started his first game post-surgery in September of 1996. The Yankees' most trusted pitcher won the swing Game 3 of the 1996 World Series in Atlanta, and he heavily contributed on-field success and off-field leadership during his tenure in New York.

In 2004, two days before baseball's highly anticipated rematch of the 2003 American League Championship Series with the Boston Red Sox, Yankees' pitcher Mariano Rivera found out that two of his wife's relatives had died in an electrical accident. Rivera helped his family grieve and make funeral arrangements in Panama before arriving back in New York in time for Game 1 of the series.

After spring training in 2007, Johnny Damon—the Yankees' center fielder and leadoff hitter who would be a catalyst for the 2009 championship team—almost quit baseball entirely while dealing with internal conflicts.

Said Damon of that time period, "I was really bummed out by the way everything ended for us in 2006 (losing to the Detroit Tigers in four games in the ALDS). [Gary Sheffield] being benched, Alex [Rodriguez] batting eighth, all of that. We'd worked so hard to have it end that way when I felt we had the best team. And then after Cory Lidle's death, I started looking at things in a bigger picture, being home with my kids after missing all the years of them growing up."

Cory Lidle was a thirty-four-year-old pitcher acquired by the Yankees in 2006. Four days after the Yankees were eliminated from that season's ALDS, Lidle was aboard a small plane with his flight instructor when the plane slammed into a forty-story building in New York City.

Lidle and his instructor were both killed in the crash. The fact that Damon felt the need to contemplate his career after Lidle's death is more than understandable, and it's a feeling that happens regularly for us all.

Before he was a member of the Yankees' formidable lineup, Giancarlo Stanton encountered one of the sport's scariest on-field injuries. Late in the 2014 season, while a member of the Miami Marlins, Stanton sustained multiple facial fractures, dental damage, and cuts that needed stitches after being hit in the face by a fastball. Stanton now wears an extended protection plate on his helmet to protect him, and many of his fellow major leaguers have followed suit as an extra safety precaution, especially with more pitchers throwing harder and faster than ever before.

When Stanton was traded to the Yankees from the Marlins, he gave an insight into the acclimation process of learning a new city, saying, "I don't know what street I'm on, what I'm wearing [for the weather], or even what I'm eating anymore."

Anyone that has ever had to move, intracity or to a completely new area, surely can relate to the time it takes to truly get settled in, much less be expected to produce at work from day one.

The *human* stories of the Yankees' past aren't told to elicit pity. Rather, they are told to highlight the incredible togetherness the teams had in tough times and the mental fortitude they had in overcoming the situations. All organizations will encounter times when their people are having difficulties that aren't directly related to work. Recognize those moments and give people the time and space they need to recover their own strength. This is important for leaders to practice, because it shows that caring extends beyond the game—to the people who play it.

Summary of *Culture*

There are people within and outside of sports who complain that free agency and player empowerment have created the wrong type of culture. Critics believe players should stick with a team no matter the environment. Oftentimes, the point that is missed by those grouches is a human one: Why would a player—*a person*—want to play for a bad organization?

It makes sense that ballplayers—*people*—didn't want to play for the Yankees in the 1980s, when they were the epitome of toxicity. In the business world, if a person is a member of a lousy corporate company, they usually don't go running home to tell family and friends to apply for a job there. Furthermore, these people are often encouraged to leave and find greener pastures.

The Yankees shed the label of a sad culture long ago and now are widely considered to be the ultimate first-class experience. Turning down a chance to play for the Yankees would be like turning down an opportunity to work at Google. Unless it's a location issue, there aren't many reasons to say "No" to being a part of what many view as the best culture in the industry.

To steal a line from the famous New Zealand All Blacks, players with the Yankees have the mindset to leave the pinstripe uniform in a better place than when they came in. That's the *culture* the Yankees have created in New York, one that is filled with *excellence* from the front office, to the major league roster, all the way down through the minor league affiliates.

Chapter Five

Player-Led Teams

Sam Walker writes in his best-selling book, *The Captain Class*, that "the most crucial ingredient in a team that achieves and sustains historic greatness is the character of the player who leads it."

This is why I'm dedicating a specific unit to player-led teams.

Studies all over the world show that player-led teams almost always outperform coach-led ones. Why? Player-led teams *take responsibility and ownership* for the pulse of the entire culture, in addition to each individual being concerned with their own development and accomplishments.

Cultures like this have players who are empowered and self-aware. These types of groups realize that, at the end of the day, it is *their* team, and the success and failure of the team are more affected by the performances of the players than by the coaches and managers.

That's not to say that coaches and managers are exempt from responsibility. They should be willing participants when it comes to culture building. But any manager or coach will admit that it's much easier to do their job when the players can police themselves.

In the early 1990s, the Yankees endured a perception problem, and their culture was still trying to recover from the toxicity of the

1980s. The easiest way to change that image and create a culture that players wanted to be a part of was to bring in *good clubhouse people*.[35]

After missing out on top-tier free agents in the early part of the 1990s, the Yankees were able to shed the destructive culture label and land top-flight players between 1992 and 1993. One of the first strokes of good luck came when the Yankees inked pitcher Jimmy Key. A considerable part of the reason Key signed is because the Yankees were bringing in people with lesser-known personalities, but players who put winning above their own personal successes.

Another aspect that helped lure some bigger fish was that the Yankees began to play better "team ball." In 1993, they won eighty-eight games, and they were in first place in 1994 before the league-wide strike wiped out the rest of the season.

The Yankees would return to the playoffs in 1995, for the first time since 1981, before winning four of the next five World Series titles, beginning in 1996.

The modern Yankee culture had arrived.

David Cone: Leader, But Not Captain

The run of success for the Yankees from 1993 to 2003 was remarkable, given what the previous decade had produced. While manager Joe Torre often receives much of the credit for the prestige restored to the franchise, it was actually one of his pitchers who became one of the most important clubhouse pieces and a major contributor to the player-led culture the Yankees had during that time period.

---

[35] Paul O'Neill and his fiery attitude were brought in for the 1993 season, via trade, and Wade Boggs, the consummate professional, signed with the Yankees after getting run out of town by the Boston Red Sox. O'Neill became a transformed player in New York, and after hitting .246 in his final season in Cincinnati, he hit .359 in 1994, winning the batting title. Boggs came to the Yankees and added to his future Hall of Fame résumé by making the All-Star team in four of his five seasons. The successes of those two acquisitions helped other players see New York as a place where they, too, could achieve at a high level.

David Cone and Torre were together for five seasons with the Yankees. Before coming to the Bronx, Cone made his name in the neighboring Queens borough with the Mets before pitching for his hometown Kansas City Royals and winning a Cy Young Award in 1994.[36]

After Torre took over the Yankees in 1996, there were two reasons the manager would continually seek Cone's advice on the clubhouse radar and leadership. The first was that Cone had handled New York in the past as a proven pitcher who could win, but also as someone who knew the intricacies of the New York media. The second reason came on the mound in Atlanta during Game 3 of the 1996 World Series.

The Yankees had lost the first two games of the series to the defending champion Braves, and with the pressure mounting to prevent a sweep, Torre turned to his savvy veteran to lead the team to a much-needed victory.

By that point in the season, Cone had already cemented a warrior-like image with the Yankee faithful; he had returned in September after undergoing surgery in May to remove an aneurysm from his right throwing shoulder. But by the sixth inning of Game 3, Cone was tiring and trying to preserve a 2–0 Yankees lead. He walked third baseman Chipper Jones to load the bases, and the Braves were threatening to end the series before it could get back to New York.

Enter Joe Torre.

In most game situations, a manager only goes out to the mound to make a pitching change. Normally, the pitching coach is tabbed to go to the mound to calm nerves or talk strategy about the opposing hitters. This was assuredly anything but a normal game situation, and there stood Torre, face-to-face with his veteran pitcher, setting up a trust or bust moment.

As Cone tells the story, Torre came just about nose-to-nose with him and implored him to be honest, asking him if he understood the significance of the game, and how he felt on the mound. Torre wanted

---

[36] Cone won the award at the expense of his future Yankees' teammate, Jimmy Key.

the truth, and he said of Cone that the pitcher never hesitated in his responses. Cone told Torre that he felt all right and that he could get the necessary outs remaining. Torre would later say that 70 or 75 percent of David Cone was better than 100 percent of someone else, because he'd "been down that road before."

That road led Cone to a stop in Seattle, Washington, one year prior, during Game 5 of the 1995 American League Division Series between the Yankees and the Mariners. At that moment, Cone was unable to preserve a 4–2 Yankees lead entering the eighth inning of the decisive game of the series, and the Yankees would lose the contest in eleven innings, their season ending in shock and bitter disappointment.

One year later in Atlanta, Cone had convinced his manager to let him give it another try. Cone wound up walking in one run to cut the lead to 2–1 before escaping the inning without further damage. That was the end of Cone's night, and the Yankees would hang on to win the swing game of the World Series, 5–2, before eventually coming back to win the series in six games.

Cone played five and a half seasons in New York, won sixty-four regular-season games, compiled a combined Wins Above Replacement (WAR) of 21.1, while also producing in clutch situations numerous times during the Yankees postseason runs from 1995 to 2000.

More importantly, Cone became a *de facto* spokesman, a position that is usually saved for an everyday player and not a starting pitcher who takes the ball every four turns. His rapport with the media allowed more quiet personalities, such as Bernie Williams and Paul O'Neill, to play without the burden of media responsibilities that typically would have fallen to them.

Cone understood, from his time with the Mets, that the reporters had to write stories, whether or not the team cooperated. As such, he wanted the columns to reflect the players' perspectives and have their spin on it, rather than give the writers too much autonomy.

As a person, Cone was known to be emotional, but he was also honest and inspirational. Cone was skillful with the media and even better when it came to *having difficult conversations*. Even the greatest teams in the best of times will encounter situations that test the leadership of people like Cone.

When Joe Girardi first came to the Yankees in 1996, he replaced a fan-favorite power-hitting catcher named Mike Stanley. Girardi was anything but a power hitter, and he struggled mightily at the plate during the early part of the 1996 season. The pressure of replacing Stanley, along with the boo birds from the Yankee Stadium crowds,[37] quickly began to mount on the new catcher.

Cone, like the Yankee brass that brought him to New York, saw Girardi as the quarterback. They didn't bring him to the Bronx to hit with the power of Mike Stanley. The Yankees wanted Girardi for his on-field leadership qualities as well as his ability to build relationships with the pitching staff, make excellent calls regarding pitch execution, and play superb defense behind the plate. That was Girardi's job.

It was Cone who reminded his first-year batterymate of this and suggested that Girardi call into New York's all-day sports-talk radio station,[38] WFAN, to address his lack of power and be honest about his struggles in replacing Stanley. After first resisting, Girardi did decide to make the call, and afterward he was finally able to relax. Angry fan calls and constant bashing from broadcasters stopped, and Girardi ended up winning three rings as a player with the Yankees.

Another example of Cone's leadership came two seasons later in the midst of a tense American League Championship Series battle with the defending league champion, Cleveland Indians. The Indians had ended the Yankees' season in the ALDS in 1997, and the Yankees were looking to right a wrong that had been simmering within them all season during 1998.

After easily winning Game 1, the Yankees looked to take a commanding lead in the series before they headed back to Cleveland

---

[37] Urban Dictionary defines "Boo Birds" as "the sound of disgust coming from a crowd at a sporting event after something they didn't like happens."
[38] "Batterymate" is a baseball term for the pairing of a pitcher and a catcher.

for Game 3. But an early Indians homer by future Yankee David Justice, and several squandered scoring opportunities for the Yankees, left Game 2 tied at one and entering extra innings. Unfortunately for the Yankees, the game would be decided after one bizarre play that swung the series temporarily in Cleveland's favor.

With nobody out in the top of the twelfth inning, the Indians dropped a bunt toward first baseman Tino Martinez, who charged the ball, gloved it, and threw to second baseman Chuck Knoblauch, who was covering first base. The ball hit the back of the Indians' runner as he stepped on the first base bag, and ended up rolling down the first base line.

It was a bang-bang play,[39] in the heat of a tense moment late in a playoff game, and instead of running over to retrieve the lost ball, Knoblauch stood at first base arguing that the runner was in the baseline, while another Indians player scored the go-ahead run to give Cleveland the lead in a game they eventually won. The win evened the series at one game apiece and helped Cleveland steal home-field advantage from the Yankees.

While it's true that Knoblauch may have had a valid point about the Indians' runner being in the baseline, the second baseman had an enormous lapse in judgment when he decided to let the ball roll down the right field line. Knoblauch compounded the situation and infuriated the media and fans when, after the game, he denied to reporters that he had done anything wrong.

Cone knew that his teammate probably didn't mean to come off as if he were in denial, but that's exactly how it was perceived. Cone also knew he needed to nip this in the bud for Knoblauch, and for the Yankees, if they were going to achieve their ultimate goals. The pitcher wouldn't let the blunder in Game 2 be the series-defining play.

On the plane on the way to Cleveland, Cone found a somber Knoblauch and grabbed him a beer so they could talk. Cone told Knoblauch about the time he was pitching for the Mets in 1990 in

---

[39] A term used to describe a close play in baseball.

Atlanta against the Braves, and two runners advanced on a play that was eerily similar to the one Knoblauch was involved in during Game 2. The teammates shared a couple of light laughs at each other's expense, and Cone recommended that Knoblauch defuse the issue immediately, saying it would lift a burden off him if he just admitted he made a mistake.

The next day, before Game 3, Knoblauch went into a room full of media members, conceded that he blew the play, and the issue was alleviated. The Yankees won the ALCS and swept the San Diego Padres in the World Series, with Knoblauch getting big hits and making sparkling defensive plays in numerous games.

David Cone's ability to connect with and influence teammates was a major factor in building the player-led teams of the Yankees' dynasty during the late 1990s. He was never officially named captain, but it's clear that without him, those teams may have underachieved due to human elements such as the pressures of playing professional baseball under the game's brightest lights.

The Captain, Part I: Don Mattingly

"If a guy wasn't doing his job or dogging it a little bit, we could get on that guy face-to-face. The guys were ready to play most of the time, but if it needed to be done—the few times—nobody had a problem on this team going to somebody else and telling them, 'Let's go. You need to do this and that.' And that player would understand.

"It didn't have to be a media thing; it didn't have to go through the writers. We handled that inside, and it was a good thing we had going."

Former first baseman Tino Martinez's quote regarding the intra-clubhouse code beautifully illustrates how powerful a player-led team can be. Many people consider the good-natured culture and player-led team types of the Yankees being born during the days of Martinez's predecessor, Don Mattingly.

Mattingly was, in essence, the bridge between the old Bronx Zoo and the new way of Yankees baseball. The former first baseman was brought up to the big leagues the year after the Yankees' 1981 World Series appearance, and he played his last game the year before the team's 1996 World Series title. While there was little good to be found in the Bronx during the majority of his time, Mattingly was one of the best players of the 1980s, winning a batting title in 1984, Most Valuable Player in 1985, and appearing in six straight All-Star games during the decade.

Mattingly was eventually named the tenth captain of the Yankees, and he held the title from 1991 until his retirement after the 1995 season. He was known by his teammates as someone who was always prepared, played the game hard, enjoyed competing, and made it easy for younger players to acclimate.

Mattingly, simply, was *a person who cared.*

Mattingly made it his responsibility to welcome incoming players from other clubs and explain the Yankees' expectations to them, while also highlighting how he thought the new player could help them win.

He could also jump on a player's case when needed, most notably that of the combustible Paul O'Neill. After making an out, O'Neill would often storm into the dugout in a rage of gloom and failure. Mattingly would lay right into the right fielder and say, "Oh, big fuckin' O'Neill, grow up. You think these people give a shit that you hit the ball on the nose at the right fielder? I don't want to hear it when you hit one off the end of the bat and it corkscrews over the third baseman's head."

Most times, Mattingly didn't feel the need to call out teammates like he did to O'Neill once in a while, but knowing he *would,* the other Yankee players held their attitudes in check.

Mattingly's final manager, Buck Showalter, had glowing reviews of the captain he inherited when he took over prior to the 1992 season. "Donnie was one of those guys who realized the weight his words carried," Showalter said. "Donnie would handle things behind the scenes. That's why [when] people say 'Well, this guy's not really vocal, not really boisterous,' [I say,] 'Do you know what goes on in a plane, in the locker room, and during a game?'

"Donnie was special," Showalter continued. "There are not many people like him. Donnie had no ego. I can sincerely say this—he equated whether or not he had a good day at the ballpark with whether or not the Yankees won."

The rosy lens through which Mattingly is remembered today was, at one point, a more serious and complicated matter. After winning salary arbitration in 1987, Mattingly quickly became the latest victim of George Steinbrenner's constant verbal attack.

The Boss blasted his best player, accusing Mattingly of being the singular reason for the Yankees' championship drought,[40] saying, "The monkey is clearly on his back. He has to deliver a championship like Reggie Jackson did. [Mattingly's] like all the rest of them now. He can't play little Jack Armstrong of Evansville, Indiana, anymore."

Unlike some players before him, Mattingly wasn't going to back down from those comments, and he shot back at the Yankees' owner through the Boss's favorite vice—the media—saying, "You come here and you play and you get no respect. They belittle your performance and make you look bad in the media. After they give you the money, it doesn't matter. They can do whatever they want. They think money is respect."

Steinbrenner was furious at the rebuttal from Mattingly, and some suggested that the first baseman's time in New York could be coming to an end. There are conflicting reports on just how close the owner actually got to trading his biggest star, but the two sides eventually reconciled, and Mattingly would be held in high esteem by Steinbrenner until the Boss passed away in July of 2010.

Longtime Yankees' broadcaster, Suzyn Waldman, once said of Steinbrenner, "You could fight with George—he liked that. He didn't want yes men around him."

By showing a willingness to stand up for himself, Mattingly laid the blueprint for the attributes that would later lead to Joe Torre and Brian Cashman establishing their own working relationships with the stormy owner of the Yankees.

---

[40] The title-less spell was *only* at eight years.

Mattingly had found a way to coexist with his hands-on boss, and he had the respect of his teammates, but winning at a high level seemed to always escape Mattingly. Even in 1985, the club's best year from a record standpoint, the Yankees won ninety-seven games, but they finished two games behind the Toronto Blue Jays in the American League East division and sat at home watching the playoffs.

The way his last few years in New York played out, and the ensuing success of the Yankees after his retirement, helped Mattingly understand the differences in his team's cultures throughout the years. "I had Billy [Martin] in there three times," Mattingly said. "When I was going through it, I just thought it was normal in New York. But when looking back, when [Buck] Showalter came in, things started to become stable. He was there [four] years before Joe [Torre] came in.

"Looking back on it now, you can't build an organization if you're going to change your manager every year. You have to have some continuity in there, someone who knows the players. And really, when it comes down to it, you're going to win with players."

By the end of Mattingly's time in New York, he could see the culture known today starting to flourish. "We started getting guys that were bothered when we lost," he said. "We cared that we lost and we started getting some character."

That character was built with help from Mattingly, who always had a no-excuses attitude toward his job. "My first game in New York was Yankee Stadium on Opening Day," Mattingly said. "I got like three plays that were all crazy. [But] you suck it up. The place is booing you, but that's just part of it. You just suck it up, and at the end you answer the questions—and you know you don't make those mistakes again.

"The way I look at it is that it's not the first mistake I've made, and it's not going to be the last. But ... it's the last time I make *that* mistake."

If there was one concept that *didn't* change over the course of Mattingly's fourteen-year career in New York, it was the *expectation* from the organization and the fan base to *win*.

"One thing you knew when you went to spring training with the Yankees was you didn't really come there just to play .500," Mattingly stated. "You didn't come there to get a little better, [either]. You want to win it all—and that was the best thing about playing in New York."

The Captain, Part II: Derek Jeter

The man who eventually succeeded Mattingly as captain of the Yankees was a player whose career was just beginning as Mattingly's came to a harsh ending in Seattle during the 1995 playoffs. Derek Jeter, like the legendary Mickey Mantle before him, seemed to be born at the right time to play for the New York Yankees. While no athlete may ever own a city quite like Mantle did in New York, there was no doubt that Jeter was king of the town during his time.

Jeter was only twenty-two years old when he earned the full-time shortstop position for the Yankees in 1996. He was far from a finished product, but many in the organization could already see the swagger that helped make him a first-round draft pick—sixth overall—in the 1992 amateur draft.

Jeter was named the eleventh captain in Yankees history on June 3, 2003. Before becoming captain, Jeter was a rookie trying to earn the trust of a team stacked with shrewd veterans like Wade Boggs, David Cone, and Paul O'Neill. His first manager, Joe Torre, quickly realized he had a legitimate on-field leader, and those seasoned players all found themselves turning to Jeter for on-field reassurance during the shortstop's first season. Most impressive was that veterans would go to Jeter with matters they felt didn't need to go all the way up the chain of command to Torre—a practice that would continue throughout Jeter's career.

His clutch performance, a signature of Jeter's game, gave him clout with the more accomplished players. He first displayed that ability by hitting a home run on Opening Day of 1996 in Cleveland. In the World Series that same season, Jeter led off the sixth inning of Game 4 and started the first of two three-run Yankee rallies to tie the game —this after being down 6–0 earlier in the game. The Yankees eventually won that game 8–6 in ten innings, won the World Series three nights later, and a star was born.

From day one, Jeter did plenty to earn the respect of his teammates, coaches, and the rest of the organization, but that didn't mean he was immune to a rookie mistake along the way. In a July 1996 game versus the Chicago White Sox, Jeter was caught attempting to steal a base, making the third out of an inning, while their big bopper, Cecil Fielder, was at the plate.

The Yankees lost that game in ten innings, and afterward, "Mr. Torre" (as Jeter affectionately referred to his boss) felt the need to teach his young superstar a lesson in accountability. "You don't trade for Cecil Fielder to take the bat out of his hands," the manager said postgame to the media. "That's a play that stunned me. Coming from him [Jeter], it really stunned me. He's a kid, and so you give him a certain amount of rope, but it's not a smart play."

After the public display of the need for accountability, Torre and Jeter quickly moved on from the moment, and the Yankees continued their winning ways.

Jeter integrated himself into a Yankees team that was built on hard work and prioritized group success over individual goals. He was easily able to integrate himself into the fold because of his acute understanding of New York and what the Yankees franchise represented, saying, "You have to be understanding of those traits to be successful in New York. One, the media. Two, confidence. Three, having fun. And four, working hard and being intense."

"And that [Yankees] mindset is," Jeter added, "do *whatever* it takes to win a game."

Jeter quickly became known in the clubhouse and in the press as someone who was true to his values and was serious about his craft. Torre was once quoted saying, "There's a certain—*cold* is too strong a word—a business mentality with him. You earn your keep with Derek."

Jeter's Yankees adopted a like-minded approach of *always* wanting to win. That's what his Yankees strived for, and as a result, they played hard and selfless for each other. The intense and confident manner Jeter wore was rooted in his philosophy of one ultimate goal each season: win the World Series. It was as if the Boss had molded the perfect Yankee and named him Derek Jeter. It would be difficult to find anyone who maniacally believed in winning the World Series each season in the same way Steinbrenner and Jeter did.

After blowing a Game 7, ninth-inning lead in the 2001 World Series, a reporter caught up to the shortstop to get his take on the season that had just cruelly ended. Jeter's response? Exactly what was expected. "You don't play to get to the World Series," he shot back at the reporter. "You play to win the World Series."

Jeter's leadership education started in 1995 with none other than Don Mattingly. From one current captain to a future one, a piece of advice Mattingly shared with Jeter was how to deal with the New York media. Mattingly wanted Jeter to know that he needed to be accountable when it came to the publicity and press aspect of playing for the Yankees, and it was Mattingly who taught Jeter how to say the right things. Jeter took the message to heart, and throughout his career he believed in being accessible to reporters in addition to being accountable for poor play. His relationship with the media could be described as distant and guarded, but he was never rude, and he would not embarrass anyone trying to do their job.

Jeter was once quoted as saying that he was *never afraid to fail.* Whether or not that was completely true was deemed irrelevant by his success on and off the field. Jeter *seemed* to be immune to failure and he *radiated confidence.* Of this attitude, Jeter once said, "People put too much pressure on themselves and try to make things bigger than they really are. No matter how you look at it, whether you're in the World Series or a spring training game, it's still baseball.

"I've gotten a hit before. I've struck out before. I've made a play. I've made an error. I mean everything that you can think of has happened to every player. It's just a matter of, are you afraid to fail? I'm not."

The selfless belief Jeter had as a Yankee was grounded in a foundation that no one person was bigger than the team. "You can't win a championship by yourself," he once said. "You can be the best player in baseball and, unless you have good people around you and a good team, it won't matter."

Stats and accolades meant little to Jeter if wins weren't racking up. That's what was special about Jeter. He didn't need flashiness, and his blue-collar approach toward the game was endearing to even the most hardened Yankee haters.

Jeter, even before being appointed, was *always* the first person out of the dugout or on the top step of it to congratulate a teammate for a job well done. He was by most measures a captain who wasn't hard to please. All he asked was that they work hard, be accountable, and have a willingness to place the team ahead of individual needs.

If Jeter thought the Yankees were acting too selfishly, he had a masterful way to address the situation, according to his former teammate Mike Mussina. "If Derek said something," the pitcher said, "we knew he was frustrated or upset or bothered by what was going on …. He wouldn't pick out anybody. It was *we* are not getting guys over. *We* are not working counts like we do when we're successful. *We* are not playing good defense. Derek understood that you had to talk like the manager, that it had to be *we* and not you."

The ability to recognize that "*we*" was more important than "*I*" is what earned Derek Jeter recognition as one of the sport's ultimate *team* competitors, and that's what made Jeter a leader that all people should model themselves after.

Being "Captain" Isn't the Only Requirement to Lead

Don Mattingly wasn't named the captain of the Yankees until his tenth season with the team, while Derek Jeter wasn't named captain until before his eighth season. Before Mattingly's appointment in 1991, the Yankees operated without a captain for two seasons; before Jeter's 2003 appointment, they went eight seasons, and the Yankees have been without an official captain since Jeter's retirement following the 2014 season.

So how does a team with no official captain, for however long a period it may be, continue to operate as player-led as the Yankees do?

It starts with the understanding that leaders and captains aren't born as such, while also realizing the impact the other core members play in keeping culture in check. Don Mattingly had Wade Boggs, Paul O'Neill, a young Bernie Williams, and David Cone who served as additional cornerstone leaders. During the dynasty years—years in which the Yankees had no official captain—they had holdovers such as O'Neill, Williams, and Cone, but also added in team-first players like Scott Brosius and David Justice.

Of course, there were the three other members of the "Core Four": Mariano Rivera, Jorge Posada, and Andy Pettitte—Yankees who, like Jeter, put winning above all else. Those Core Four players achieved credibility with their teammates by consistently showing up day-in-day-out, and year-in-year-out, with the same blue-collar, workmanlike attitude. This approach helped them win four World Series titles in five seasons, but also helped them establish long and successful careers. With those four players, it was impossible to know if it was 1996, 2003, or 2011 because each of them operated as though they hadn't yet won or achieved anything.

The years since the last championship for the Yankees have still seen players with team-first leadership come through. That has allowed their sustainability to continue even in the face of turnover and adversity. Those players have all filled the role of leader and taken on the responsibility of upholding the Yankees' excellence, even if the clubs they played on may not have been on par with those of the past.

A person willing to take on the serious responsibilities of a leader during the rough patches stands out more than those who accepted their roles when everything was going right. But the point is not to diminish one versus the other; the purpose is to say that leadership really does come in all shapes and forms. It is needed in good situations and bad ones, too.

The Future Captain: Aaron Judge

In keeping with the brand, the Yankees' unspoken leader of present-day does not have the label *captain* associated with his name. The man who can lay claim to his own section in the Yankee Stadium outfield seats, Aaron Judge, might as well have been molded as a replica of Derek Jeter.

Judge has a placid demeanor, but a serious internal will to win and succeed. Judge is more physically imposing than Jeter (and pretty much anyone else in baseball), but he flashes the same *aw-shucks* smile that Jeter perfected, and has quickly earned the hearts of Yankee fans.

Like Jeter, Judge can seemingly go from "easy-going" to "fire in his eyes" with a snap of the fingers. Jeter used to chat with the young kids sitting behind the on-deck circle before walking to the plate and collecting one of his 3,465 hits; from his right field position, Judge likes to play catch with youthful fans in the stands between innings, before playing extraordinary defense during a game.

Jeter and Judge shared an innocence for a game that is loved by children, but can be a grind for adults. And, like Jeter, Judge's journey toward his unofficial label began in the minor leagues. This is where his former manager, Joe Girardi, first noticed Judge's impact on the other Yankee prospects. A new, cohesive feel was being built, largely through the young Judge's influence. General Manager Brian Cashman echoed that sentiment, saying, "I think he's been extremely professional in how he's gone about his business, the focus being on baseball. One thing Judge has always had is high leadership qualities throughout our minor leagues that were very similar to Derek Jeter's qualities."

Judge was called up to the majors for his first game on August 13, 2016, and he greeted Yankee fans everywhere with a bang, blasting his first career home run in his first career at-bat. An injury would cut short most of the rest of Judge's first season in the majors, but he had done enough on the field and in the clubhouse to warrant getting a shot as the full-time right fielder in 2017.

The Yankees' faith in Judge was immediately rewarded as he was named AL Rookie of the Month in April 2017. By season's end, Judge had embarked on a historic freshman campaign; his fifty-two homers set a new Major League rookie record and smashed the Yankees' rookie record of twenty-nine, held since 1936 by the legendary Joe DiMaggio.

Most importantly, the Yankees were winning and back in the playoffs.

Since his breakout season, Judge has become a household name in baseball and has led the Yankees to three straight playoff appearances. He won the AL Rookie of the Year Award in 2017 and finished a close second in the MVP voting that same season.

Preparation is at the foundation of Judge's leadership style. "I'm big into preparing," the right fielder says. "I don't like being unprepared for things, so in my mind I went through all the different scenarios, what's going on for tomorrow and the next day."

His teammate Brett Gardner thinks that Judge's most impressive work takes place off the field and that the youngster brings a positive attitude to the stadium each day.

Judge knows how to pick his battles when trying to right a wrong. "I want to lead by example," he says. "But I also want the best out of my teammates. If I see something, I'm going to say it, but not on the field when emotions are full."

That's leadership: Knowing that something needs to be said, but being perceptive enough to understand the appropriate time to deliver it.

Judge also knows that he doesn't have to do this alone. He's had his own mentors, such as CC Sabathia and Gardner. Of Sabathia, Judge says, "Whether you had ten years in or you were just called up, he's gonna show you respect. The way he treats people is amazing."

Judge will be with the team long after Sabathia—who retired after the 2019 season—and Gardner are gone. But the "good guy" selfless leadership made standard by those players will be carried on by Judge for years to come.

While a championship still eludes the Yankees' leader, there is no doubt that he is the man they have given their full support to, and it's a challenge that Judge is up to taking. By staying even-keeled, a trait he says he learned from Jeter, the Yankees have a player in Judge that can lead them into a new decade and continue nurturing the Yankees' culture that was built before him.

Summary of *Player-Led Teams*

Player-led teams are a key component to achieving a *Culture of Excellence*. It's safe to say that without the player-led culture, the Yankees may not have achieved the sustainable success that continues to be a part of their DNA.

A player-led team can put out a fire before it goes full-blaze or make in-game adjustments when a predetermined strategy goes off the rails. Player-led teams take responsibility and ownership, and they are empowered and self-aware.

Thus, one can conclude that players who lead aren't all that different from coaches, managers, or executives. But they *are* the ones in the trenches, and that's what makes their ability to influence so vital. Teams that win understand this methodology and ensure that they focus their leadership responsibilities on the ones playing the game, and not just toward the people that watch it.

Chapter Six

Community

W e are all part of a community, in our careers and in life, but whether or not we are contributing members of that community is a whole different ball game.

If the *Culture* pillar is built upon two aspects, people and community, then the *people* in our *communities* need to foster an excellent working and living experience. When done right, the package deal will enhance our leadership and organizational reputations.

Reinventing the Yankee Stadium Experience

The House That George Built was in need of innovation toward the start of the twenty-first century's second decade.[41] After the Core Four's—Derek Jeter, Mariano Rivera, Andy Pettitte, and Jorge Posada—final run came to a gloomy end in 2012, ticket sales dropped sharply, as did the fan interest in the on-field product.

One of the main issues concerning the Yankee brass was the lack of interest from millennial supporters. Even during the team's revival from 2009 to 2012, the millennial connection had been down.

This, of course, is not a Yankees-specific problem, nor is it a baseball-specific issue. Fans across all sports now have more access to

---

[41] A nickname given to the current-day Yankee Stadium, representing the importance of George Steinbrenner.

teams than ever before via sources such as online streaming and social media. In addition to that, ticket sales drop-offs can be attributed to a better viewing experience at home, and the inability for spectators to spend hundreds of dollars on tickets and concessions.

Owner Hal Steinbrenner took stock of a home crowd one day during the mid-2010s and decided radical change was in order for the stadium his father helped build.

Steinbrenner's vision for improving optics at Yankee Stadium closely resembled his game plan for his on-field product: *the future.* The new Yankees owner paid an agency for a study to see what millennials wanted at ball games, and the results of the examination told Steinbrenner that prospective fans wanted an *experience.*

Jason Zillo, the Yankees' Vice President of Communications and Media Relations, said of the needed transformation, "It's all part of a shift towards making the experience more interactive. It's a different era. It's a different group of fans. Fans are looking for things on their trip to a stadium that fans weren't looking for ten years ago, twenty years ago, thirty years ago."

Take, for example, Atlanta's Truist Park. The ballpark, home to the Braves, opened in 2017, and is state-of-the-art in regard to aesthetics, food, and amenities. Outside the park there is a neighborhood feel, with plenty of bars and restaurants for socializing. Inside, besides ziplining and great between-innings entertainment, there are plenty of food and drink options—traditional and non—and get this: It is all *reasonably priced*, attracting folks of all demographics and with all types of needs and wants.

The old status quo of going to a ball game to watch *only* the on-field action isn't enough anymore. Fans young and old, but especially young, want to document their time at the ballpark on Snapchat, Facebook, and Instagram. The Yankees needed to enhance the stadium experience to have a chance at increasing ticket sales—regardless of whether or not they have a winning team on the field.[42]

The aftermath of the millennial study altered the structure of the new Yankee Stadium. Steinbrenner had a crew of workers put selfie stations all around the park, and the concourse area overlooking Monument Park was reconstructed into a gigantic outdoor bar. It's a common sight now for that area of the stadium to be filled with people of all ages socializing, posing for social media pictures, and holding a drink or food in hand. Better yet, millennial attendance has increased each season at Yankee Stadium since 2017.

In addition to the aesthetics facelift, and at Steinbrenner's insistence, in-game spots for Yankees' minor leaguers were created for the video board. This was done so that fans in the Bronx could see the future Yankees and have familiarity with the prospects before they arrive in New York.

In 2017, the franchise premiered *Homegrown: The Path to Pinstripes*, a reality television series on the YES Network. The program showcases the next generation of Yankee players and follows the on and off-field developments of some of the organization's top prospects.

---

[42] This author is a fan who was lucky enough to be a recipient of one of the more recent game experiences. While attending an early July game in 2017, for a late Father's Day gift, our crew was at the stadium early, primarily to watch rookie-phenom Aaron Judge take batting practice. We were also about three rows from the final row in the third deck along the first base line when a young lady approached us with the offer of a lifetime: the Yankees employee told us they walk around the upper deck to find groups of two or four people (we had four) and offer them a seat upgrade as part of a Mohegan Sun partnership.

We happily accepted the upgrade, even if it meant sitting in the sweltering sun for more than three hours, and we were introduced on the big screen to the Saturday crowd before first pitch.

The date was July 8, 2017, and the *experience* turned up another notch for us when the Yankees won the game 5–3, on a three-run walk-off home run by left fielder, Clint Frazier. It's impossible to make up that story, and it will forever be a memory, one that we might not have had if we'd been stuck in the upper deck for the entire game.

Innovation was needed to bring life back to Yankee Stadium. Sure, winning helps, but creating a ballpark experience that is *inclusive of all people* and not just die-hard Yankee fans is the ultimate winner here.

Credit Hal Steinbrenner for having the foresight to see this and make it a reality.

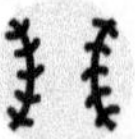

The House That Ruth Built is no more,[43] but its place in the Bronx community will be present for years to come, thanks to great engineering by the Yankees. On the site of the old Yankee Stadium now sits a series of baseball fields, handball courts, basketball courts, and soccer fields. The area is now known as Heritage Field, and it is used by countless children each day.

Among the ten-acre lot of fields is a baseball diamond that sits in almost the exact same spot as the original Yankee Stadium. How cool is it for kids to grow up and play baseball, standing in the same area as legends like Babe Ruth or Derek Jeter?

A twelve-ton chunk of the old Yankee Stadium frieze has been preserved in one corner of the field. Another stadium memento is the 130-foot-high chimney that's shaped like a baseball bat.[44] Generations of fans at the old Yankee Stadium met around the bat before venturing in to see the Yankees play.

To be clear, the Yankees did not have to build a multi-purpose field for the community. Many historic arenas, such as Chicago's Comiskey Field, have been turned into parking lots. Another park, Minnesota's Metropolitan Stadium, was turned into a shopping mall.

Yuck.

Heritage Park, while it didn't serve all the political issues associated with the building of the current Yankee Stadium, is now a

---

[43] A nickname given to the old Yankee Stadium, representing the importance of Babe Ruth.

[44] And *my* favorite.

place where community residents can come together, be active, and remember the fond Yankees moments of yesteryear.

9/11

September 11, 2001, was America's twenty-first-century version of Pearl Harbor. After the Pearl Harbor attack, United States President Franklin Roosevelt said to the nation, on December 7, 1941, that it was "a date which will live in infamy."

For those who were alive, 9/11 is a day that is remembered in much the same way. In 2001, as America and New York City tried their best to pull out of the rubble caused by the four terrorist attacks on the warm and sunny September morning, the nation desperately looked for anything to help bring back normalcy.

The Yankees were in the middle of another run to a World Series in 2001. But there would be no baseball in the immediate aftermath of 9/11. Instead, the franchise found itself in a unique position: that of uniters to help the nation heal.

New York City—one of the three targets of the attacks—was in particular need of a pick-me-up. "Just imagine Manhattan with no cars," Derek Jeter said at the time. "Just people walking the streets. It was like it was a movie set."

On September 15, thirteen Yankees—including their manager, Joe Torre— visited families of missing victims. Among others, Jeter, Bernie Williams, Paul O'Neill, and Mariano Rivera were part of the group that went to "Ground Zero," visited with rescue workers at Javits Center, and comforted burn victims at St. Vincent's Hospital.

At the insistence of their leader, Jeter, the Yankees chose not to make a public event out of their "Good Samaritan" act. They weren't looking to be saviors, they just wanted to help in any small way they could. "We're not here to save civilization," Torre said of their efforts. "But our job is to relieve some tension and give everyone something to enjoy."

The nation needed to move on, and baseball needed to be played to finish out the 2001 season. The Yankees responded to the moment by advancing to the playoffs where they met the scary Oakland Athletics, who boasted the reigning Most Valuable Player and future Yankee, Jason Giambi.

The Yankees dropped the first two games of the series in New York, and it seemed as though their dynasty and place as city healer were close to the end. But the team rebounded; Jeter made his famous flip play in Game 3, and back home in the Bronx the crowd roared and gave life to the Yankees. They eventually prevailed to win Game 5 and the American League Division Series.

In the American League Championship Series, the Yankees took care of the record-breaking Seattle Mariners in five games. With the Yankees dominating the series, they looked poised to handle the Arizona Diamondbacks en route to their fourth straight championship.[45] It seemed as though divine spirits were willing the Yankees to another title.

It is said that Game 7 is the greatest spectacle in sports. It's a do-or-die atmosphere where everything and everyone is on the line. Mariano Rivera and the Yankees headed out to the field only three outs away from securing a fourth consecutive championship and delivering home to New York a much-needed distraction from the realities of life.

The truth of this series was that the Yankee Stadium ghosts did not make the trip from the Bronx to the desert in Arizona. After taking a 2–1 lead in the eighth inning of Game 7, the Yankees failed to close out the Diamondbacks—who scored two runs in the bottom of the ninth to defeat the dynastic Yankees and win the World Series.

---

[45] After dropping the first two games of the World Series in Arizona, the Yankees bounced back to win Game 3 in New York. In Games 4 and 5, the ghosts of Yankee Stadium reappeared, as the Yankees held off the Diamondbacks two separate times in games where they were down two runs with two outs in the bottom of the ninth inning. Tino Martinez tied it in Game 4 with a two-run blast, before Derek Jeter sent a baseball over the wall for a home run, the first ever in the month of November, to win the game. Less than twenty-four hours later, Scott Brosius gave everyone in the crowd a glimpse into *Groundhog Day* by smashing another ninth inning, two-out, two-run homer, before the Yankees won the game in twelve innings and took a 3–2 series lead back to Arizona.

It was a thrilling seven-game "Fall Classic"[46] with moments that are still talked about fondly among fans of the game. Although the Yankees didn't win a World Series for their grieving city they acted as unifiers and helped temporarily lift the gloom in the aftermath of 9/11—both as baseball players *and* as *caring citizens* of their community.

Baseball is a game that unites a community. It doesn't take reeling from terrorist attacks to come together. Baseball brings people together during simpler and more peaceful times. It's why millions of people come out to celebrate with parades when their city's team brings home a title. Togetherness is one of the most powerful aspects of sports.

In the aftermath of 9/11, the Yankees served as more than a baseball team. It wasn't a situation that any of them asked for, but the grace and leadership that the club displayed on the field was transferred to the devastated streets of New York and gave hope to the people of their community.

Derek Jeter knows a thing or two about giving people hope.

Victor Saracini was one of the pilots on United Flight 175, the Los Angeles–bound airplane that struck the South Tower of the World Trade Center on September 11, 2001. Saracini's daughter, Brielle, was only ten years old when she found out her father had been killed.

A Yankee enthusiast and fan of Derek Jeter, Brielle Saracini wrote to Jeter three days after the terrorist attacks. "As you have heard, there was a horrible accident that involved the Twin Towers, there was a hijacking on a plane. Terrible people are in this world, but you and I both know that! Out of respect I would love it if you would pay me a visit because that horrible hijacking happened to be my father. My father was the pilot, Captain Victor J. Saracini. My family is experiencing pain that comes and goes ... My dad was a great father to me and he would want me to concur [sic] my dream, meeting you ..."

---

[46] A nickname given to the World Series, which is played each October.

Jeter, being the person he is, received the letter and immediately reached out to the grieving child. He invited the Saracini family to Yankee Stadium for a game, and spent time before and after it with Brielle, her sister, and her mother. Bonus: the Yankees won the game 3–1, behind a Derek Jeter double.

Brielle Saracini and her family have maintained a friendship with Jeter in the years following 9/11. "I'm one of the lucky few to have a special connection with him," Brielle said. "He's so much more than a baseball player to me. He's a mentor. He's someone I look up to because of the way he treats people. He is someone who has helped me through a lot of dark times."

Monument Park and Old Timer's Day

The current version of baseball is vastly different from prior generations, when the majority of players *did* play their entire career with one team. This closely resembles early twentieth century industrial and corporate America, where a high percentage of the workforce stayed with one company for careers spanning thirty or forty years, which often culminated with a gift of a gold watch upon retirement. Just as free agency changed the landscape in baseball, the open market in America has made it so that companies are seeing turnover at a far higher rate than they did in the past.

The concept that an employee will spend their whole working life in one place is as extinct as the dinosaurs. But that doesn't mean companies and their leaders accept this new practice. In fact, there are plenty of executive leaders who worry excessively about turnover. This is a noble quality to have; employers should always want to retain employees—especially high performers.

Unfortunately, a lot of these same leaders have an extremely difficult time accepting the loss of an employee, to the point that they forget how important honoring their past contributions could be toward growing the business in the future. They get so caught up with *why* an employee leaves that they lose sight of *how*.

An overlooked opportunity of any organization is the willingness to tout past employees, whether or not they were there for life. No matter the reason for leaving, more employers should consider highlighting their great performers of the past, while also pointing toward successes that these people achieved with new employers, or if they've ventured out on their own.

What's wrong with telling future employees, "We produced one of the best in the biz, and they are now off on a fresh venture, separate from ours, but one that we completely support, and we hope to see more of our employees follow a similar path"?

Think of the reaction that an employer would get from a prospective candidate in this scenario—they would be *stunned*. In a world where interviews are completely scripted by robots and Google, it would make employers stand out ten-fold from their competitors.

The New York Yankees are an excellent representation of the practice of honoring their past. In every form of media ever invented, there are ample accounts of the Yankees' glorious history.

This is a great recruiting tool for general manager Brian Cashman—he can tell prospective Yankees that they can continue to build on the excellence of people like Babe Ruth, Mickey Mantle, Joe Torre, and George Steinbrenner. Countless players over the years have expressed how impactful wearing Yankee pinstripes was to their decision-making process and career aspirations. Sure, recounting people's past success isn't necessarily a deal-breaker tactic one way or another, but it certainly doesn't hurt to do it.

The Yankees honor their brightest stars of the past in an area of Yankee Stadium called Monument Park. To date, thirty-seven former Yankees have been honored in the museum, with either a plaque or a monument, the latter of which is reserved only for the immortals—former manager Miller Huggins; former players Lou Gehrig, Babe Ruth, Mickey Mantle, and Joe DiMaggio; and former owner George Steinbrenner.

The first monument, belonging to Huggins, the manager who led the franchise to its first three championships, was dedicated in 1932. Oddly enough, it was placed out in center field at the original Yankee Stadium, up next to the "461 FT." numbers on the wall, and thus it stood in the field of play. Fans can recall video footage of the Yankees' former center fielder, Bobby Murcer, miss-playing a ball hit over his head and rolling past him and the monuments—by then, Huggins had been joined by Gehrig, and later by Ruth—and having to run between two of the monuments in order to retrieve the ball.

(The ball never actually went behind the monuments, much to Murcer's dismay, because he tried to slip through the monuments to retrieve a ball that wasn't there, but such was the life of a Yankee fan in the late 1960s and early 1970s.)

When Yankee Stadium was remodeled in the mid-1970s, the center field wall was pulled in to allow for the monuments and flagpole to stand out of the field of play. After originally being inaccessible to fans, the modern concept of Monument Park began in 1985. When the new Yankee Stadium was built for the 2009 season, the team moved all of the old artifacts across the street, and the site has become a fan favorite over the years—visited by millions each season, before the start of games.

To some, it may seem too flashy—excessive in appetite—but the purpose Monument Park serves for the Yankees' fans is undeniable and the honor former Yankees have when they are inducted is invaluable.

The franchise wants their biggest and brightest stars to be remembered for their past contributions, and that becomes another value-add to future Yankees: If players want to end up in Monument Park, they know the measuring stick. Now it's up to them to do the work.

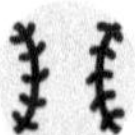

There is a true influence in honoring people from the past. The Yankees take this practice one step further than most in their industry and annually host an event they christened "Old Timer's Day" (OTD).

The first OTD wasn't held by the organization until 1947.[47] They had, however, previously executed a hugely successful appreciation day for one of the game's larger-than-life stars.

On July 4, 1939, the Yankees held "Lou Gehrig Appreciation Day" at Yankee Stadium, two months after the "Iron Horse" removed himself from the lineup. Gehrig had played in an incredible 2,130 straight games to that point, but by early 1939, he had begun to suffer from the effects of amyotrophic lateral sclerosis (ALS), a progressive neurodegenerative disease—one that would eventually bear his name.

A sold-out crowd at Yankee Stadium witnessed Gehrig give the baseball version of Abraham Lincoln's "Gettysburg Address." At the conclusion of the "Luckiest Man on the Face of the Earth" speech, the crowd, who knew of Gehrig's terminal diagnosis, roared for their fallen ballplayer. Babe Ruth and most of the 1927 "Murderers' Row" Yankees were in attendance and on the field with Gehrig. The *New York Times* reported that the occasion was "one of the most touching scenes ever witnessed on a ball field."

In the following years, there were various modest attempts to keep bringing back the Yankees alum, especially while Ruth was still alive. Ruth was a figure who was exploited for marketing purposes by early twentieth century America and the entire sport of baseball. But the Yankees had dibs on the "Sultan of Swat," and Ruth, for the most part, was happy to give back to his former employer.

When it became clear that Ruth's health was failing, talks began of recreating an event like Gehrig's appreciation day. In stepped Larry MacPhail, at the time an executive with the Yankees and the man most often credited with officially creating the concepts of OTD.

Throughout the years, OTD has served as a day where players can once again be remembered for their past contributions to the Yankees. It's also a day to see familiar friends from work, to reminisce about the past, and to meet current Yankees players. The present

---

[47] The Yankees established the same season as the American League—1903.

group loves seeing the former Yankees, and for the old timers, it's an opportunity to put the pinstripe uniform on again, even if just for a day.

With a spring training–like feel to the ceremony and game, OTD is rooted much deeper in nostalgia than it is in which group wins—the Clippers or the Bombers.[48] Fans of the past will remember famous broadcaster Mel Allen, the original master of ceremonies, introducing the Yankee players up and down the first and third base lines.

The day has also come with its own memorable on-field moments. In 1973, the final season at the original Yankee Stadium, Hall of Fame pitcher Whitey Ford served up a meatball for his old pal, Mickey Mantle, and Mantle belted the final home run of his lifetime. More recently, in 2019, Mariano Rivera pitched (his customary position), played center field, and hit an inside-the-park home run. When he was still alive, Joe DiMaggio was always introduced as the final member of OTD and as "baseball's greatest living player."

The Yankees are a team. Fans of the club and of the sport will always remember the players who added to the franchise's folklore, but OTD gives special recognition to the players who aren't in Monument Park or in baseball's Hall of Fame in Cooperstown.

The Yankees' OTD is a special occasion that highlights the amazing accomplishments of legends and supporting players. That's the most influential aspect of the idea and is the *finest* version of the Yankees' honoring their past. More organizations should seriously consider their own form of recognition to former employees.

HOPE Week

According to the Yankees' official website, yankees.com, "the Yankees' HOPE Week initiative (Helping Others Persevere and Excel) is rooted in the fundamental belief that acts of goodwill provide hope and encouragement to more than just the recipient of the gesture."

---

[48] These are two common Yankees nicknames, with the Clippers being named after Joe DiMaggio, who was also known as the "Yankee Clipper," and the Bombers pays tribute to the team's legacy as the "Bronx Bombers."

The community initiative—first spearheaded prior to the 2009 season by Yankees brass that included manager Joe Girardi and GM Brian Cashman—is a great way for the people of the franchise to get away from the ballpark and do meaningful work together.

The team picks out one home week each season to honor recipients of the award. Nominations come from a mix of ballots via yankees.com, fan mail, and independent canvassing. Each game day, the Yankees highlight a different individual, family, or organization worthy of recognition and support.

The week is designed so honorees can share their inspirational stories with Yankee players, fans, and the media. The best part of HOPE Week is that the guest(s) of honor don't know they are being treated to the special surprise until the Yankees show up. Their distinguished day then caps with a trip to Yankee Stadium.

The Yankees want HOPE Week to be about *people helping people*. They believe that—no matter where they come from, what their financial situation is, or what kind of skills they possess—everyone has time to give. Equally significant during HOPE Week: The highlighted organizations get much-needed publicity to create interest, awareness, and funding for their causes, which can be a great challenge, especially for non-profits. The Yankees also provide each honoree with media avenues to record and tell their story, a bonus feature that goes a long way in hearing the story, but also in being able to relive it.

What else does HOPE Week entail? Honorees join players and coaches during batting practice before the game and on the field after victories for celebratory high fives, they get to throw out the ceremonial first pitch, and they get to walk to home plate and exchange the lineup card—first instituted at the insistence of Girardi while he was the manager. The Yankees reward good people by giving them a day that kids for generations have dreamed of being a part of.

The HOPE Week fraternity is a strong group, too. Alumni from prior years are invited back to celebrate with the current year's honorees and form relationships that stretch far beyond their special day. Past honorees include a couple that mentors at-risk young people in Washington Heights; a non-profit that bakes and sells chocolate chip cookies during the holidays and uses the proceeds to fund all-expenses-paid vacation for families of children with life-threatening illnesses; and a college-aged volunteer organization that visits sick children in hospitals, schools, and social service institutions and gives the youngsters their "Moment of Magic"—the volunteers arrive dressed as princesses and superheroes from kids movies.

The impact HOPE Week has had on the Yankees and the world simply cannot be measured in dollars and cents. One of the most amazing developments to come from the initiative is the people and the institutions that followed suit.

In baseball, the Minnesota Twins established their own HOPE Week in 2011, and in 2014, Southern Boulevard School elementary school in Chatham Township, New Jersey, also began similar projects to give back to their communities. One can see that being a billion-dollar corporation is not a requisite for giving back.

HOPE Week has become an event that fans look forward to every season. The Yankees involve all of their players and coaches in the initiative, and by doing so, they send a message that everyone can give of themselves to make their community a better place.

Summary of *Community*

Community is more than just giving back in a charitable way, although the Yankees do an excellent job of that aspect with HOPE Week. Community involves enhancing an experience, which means doing research and being innovative. Community also lies within the idea of being inclusive for all people and being caring citizens who help one another.

If an organization like the Yankees—more storied than most—won't hang on the coattails of its past, then it's a pretty good bet that we can all stand to improve our collective communities and the experiences they entail.

As a community, we can also honor those of our present *and* past, and we can bring relief in times of need. It goes without saying that if there is a great community, then there are *even better people* who support it.

KEY POINTS: CULTURE—PEOPLE AND COMMUNITY

If a culture isn't centered around its *people*, then it is doomed to fail, no matter how talented the surrounding people may be, or how much money is being invested into the business. Exhibiting a people-first culture says to fellow humans that there is *care* involved, an attribute that may be the single most overlooked aspect of any organization.

What else is culture? The Yankees taught us it is:

- *Preparation*
- *Innovation*
- *Experience*
- *Taking responsibility and ownership*
- *Empowerment and self-awareness*
- *Being inclusive of all people*
- *People helping other people*

These qualities make up an environment that is exciting and invites success to be part of the process. Use these features as a guide toward a strong foundation that will lead to desired results and an atmosphere that people want, continually, to be a part of.

PILLAR THREE

PLAYER DEVELOPMENT AND ORGANIZATIONAL STRUCTURE

Development *(noun)* - the state of being created or made more advanced

"A lot of times, guys put a label on a person without letting the person develop. There's always people that are going to doubt you. At the end, it's up to you how hard you want to work."
- *Didi Gregorius*

Chapter Seven

Scouting and Drafting

The fluidity of business makes it nearly impossible to find a balance between success and failure, and this is why in all industries, it's common to see a company extremely skewed one way or the other. There are Fortune 500 companies that stabilize the economy, and there are start-ups that can't hang on to a dozen employees at a time and are burning through cash equity.

In baseball, the economics of today's game makes it so that the best franchises—the ones with the deepest pockets—assist in keeping small-market teams afloat.

Player and organizational development is the most difficult pillar to achieve. Oftentimes, the *people* involved are lost in the dollars and cents of business. A company—or a baseball team—doesn't stand a chance at succeeding if they can't figure out a way to find, develop, and retain talent.

Using Data and Information, Part I: Making Decisions on Talent

The job of a major league front office is to answer three main questions:

1. *Where to find money*
2. *How to spend the money*
3. *Whom to spend the money on*

Time and time again, the sport is finding itself being more *objective* about baseball players and far less *subjective* than at any point in baseball's history. The rise of analytical acumen in the game has meant that all clubs have a better understanding of the value of players, whether they are established veterans with a track record or prospects looking to get to the major leagues for the first time.

The million-dollar question on the minds of all baseball executives is one to which the answer is most elusive: *How does a team find great players in the first place, and can it find new ones to replace the ones they lose through free agency or because of age and injury?*

It is baseball lore that drafting poorly is considered a million-dollar mistake. Despite the potential debt that can result from a bad pick, executives wholeheartedly believe that the draft should *not* be a crapshoot. As such, the ability to rethink baseball—how and why it's played, what players are best suited to compete, and which coaches and managers have the greatest ability to lead—has led to a revolution.

The most significant change is related to on-field strategies and player evaluations that are being conducted by an analysis of historical statistical data, rather than by a collection of experienced baseball people and their intuition. The naked eye and pure "gut" decisions are no longer adequate tools for determining what's needed to evaluate all the aspects of baseball.

There are more non-former players in baseball front offices than ever before, and these new-age executives see the market for baseball players like stocks and bonds. The market is *always* changing, and in order to scout, draft, trade, and sign players, teams *must* be willing to be adaptable and innovative.

All teams, even clubs like the Yankees that have financial advantages, build their rosters through the draft. But on average it will take at least five years for most draft picks to become established at the major league level. So, the return on investment isn't immediate; executives, scouts, and coaches need to display patience, while also understanding that the draft is an inexact process.

Baseball, more than most sports, is a game of *skill*. The analytical revolution has seen young players with incredible physical skill levels make an impact like never before in baseball history. But player evaluation is more than just short term—the sport's executives also want to know that when a player reaches an age of physical decline, they can find a way to maintain their skill level.

This is important, because although the sport continues to trend younger each season, general managers know there aren't enough players in the pool to supplement a competitive full and active roster for *every* ball club. There is still a great need for players who can display longevity in their careers, whether or not their *value* remains the same in their later years as it did with previous generations.

Data analysis has helped regulate these outcomes on a more consistent basis than in the past. For example, it's now known that the ability to get on base frequently (requiring patience and discipline at the plate) is a skill that's *more likely* to stay with a player throughout the deteriorating-skill phase of their career, than is an extraordinary ability to hit home runs.

One only has to look at the career of a player like Ken Griffey Jr. to see this narrative as true.[49] When Griffey Jr. was a younger player, he was a major power threat, but as he got older his power numbers greatly diminished, for various reasons. However, even with decreasing power numbers, according to a study compiled by FanGraphs, Griffey Jr. was an "above average" player in all seasons in which his on-base percentage was higher than .340.

Research and quantitative data analysis show Griffey Jr. as a rule and not as an outlier. Now that on-base percentage is one proven method for long-term excellence, it is being seen as an attribute that

---

[49] From 1989 to 2000, Griffey Jr. *averaged* thirty-seven homers per season, but from 2001—his age thirty-one season—until his retirement in 2010, he only averaged nineteen long balls per season, as injuries and increasing age severely depleted his raw power skill. Griffey Jr. hit 438 of his 630 career homers during his first twelve seasons in the big leagues. During the second half of his Hall of Fame career, while his power numbers stumbled, he was able to maintain an on-base percentage above .350 in all but three of those seasons.

is imperative to the skillset of a major league prospect, and it is considered more important *and more accurate* than, say, the traditional batting average stat.

Other points of analysis have helped to further break down the barrier between intuition and information. The debate between picking a college player versus a high school player is one that has been drawn out like the old adage of what came first, the chicken or the egg? But now there are years of data and larger sample sizes showing that college players play more games against stiffer competition than their high school counterparts, so stats and evidence from the college amateurs are more accurate than those from players in high school. In relation, data says that high school pitchers are two times less likely than college pitchers and four times less likely than college position players to make it to the majors.

Where there is now evidence to help scouts and front offices determine potential skill durability for hitters, pitching analysis is fast catching up. The baseball landscape is littered with teams that control their pitchers' usage based on a pitch count, which is hardly the only factor for success, but certainly a good starting measuring tool.

If players are measured against pitch count, then teams should be looking at prospects who can throw strikes. Data supports this theory and shows that the ability to control the strike zone is the *greatest* indicator for future success. It's pretty simple: If a pitcher can control the zone, they will throw fewer pitches, therefore allowing them to (hypothetically) stay in the game longer, and have less wear and tear on their greatest asset—their throwing arm.

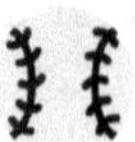

Baseball is increasingly obsessed with efficiency and value. It's true that analytics requires data, but to make it work takes *smart human implementation*. Increasingly, teams and players are adopting a growth mindset to the overarching approach of information implementation.

In addition to helpful data, teams are also more willing than they were in the past to call up young players. There's much less of an acceptance policy in place, as coaches and players want the best people to help them win—a major change from the hazing and boot-camp days rookies used to endure.

Clubs that are resistant to the analytical adaptations will find themselves with rosters depleted of depth *and* talent capable of contributing at the major league level. Just ask the Baltimore Orioles, who were one of the last adopters of analytics and have finished dead last in the American League East from 2017 to 2019.

We are only in the beginning stages of the information age, and because of that, scouting and drafting stand as some of the biggest areas to gain more knowledge than ever before. Using data to get draft picks *right* will become a best practice, because looming larger than ever before is the slimmest margin for error in selecting prospects who turn into serviceable major leaguers.

In today's game, scouting and drafting are the foundation from which all organizational philosophy derives. If a team can't get it right from the start, then they stand no real chance to compete.

Summary of *Scouting and Drafting*

Scouting and drafting—the talent acquisition of baseball—will always be a crucial foundational aspect of assembling a competitive roster. It's important to have processes in place that can evaluate prospects so that the finite resources available don't go to waste.

Because it's extremely difficult (some say impossible) to project a player into the future, it's imperative to have an operation that can determine the differentiating levels of priorities when it comes to specific skill sets. Getting this part of the equation wrong can lead to mediocrity or severe setbacks, which means people potentially losing their jobs. Using data and software to make more correct decisions should be a best practice. Information helps to stay grounded in fact-finding, while also building a stronger business case for a particular person or concept.

Talent acquisition shouldn't be a crapshoot. Take the time on the front end to get it right, and the results will positively drive an organization forward. Neglect the time to get it right on the front end, and the wheels will keep spinning, but without making any progress.

Chapter Eight

Development Isn't Always Linear

Our potential is one element, but what we do with it is quite another.

Imagine being a teenager in a third-world country where the only chance of escaping poverty is to sign a minor league contract, move to America alone, inherit the expectations of a fan base that's constantly hungry for success, and still find yourself more than a handful of years away from even getting a taste of big-league action.

Envision another scene where a twenty-one-year-old American-born athlete is drafted in the first round, inherits those same expectations from the same fan base, and is expected to contribute at the major-league level within a couple of years.

Is it possible to conceive of the pressure involved in being a professional athlete? And let's be fair: Outside of the bonuses given for the higher drafted American-born players, no player in minor league baseball is rich and famous through the lens in which spectators generalize athletes these days. Sure, the foreign-born players may have more money than they are accustomed to for the time being, but they deal with the isolation of being hundreds, if not thousands, of miles from family for long periods of time.

When talking about player development, it's important to remember the biggest piece of the puzzle: *the human element*.

In the past, athletes were treated as property. Do the work, don't complain, take what is given, and be happy with the circumstances.

From the outside, that deal may seem legitimate given the salaries they earn, but players aren't properties, and they aren't robots—even if they are expected to give 100 percent every day, no matter what the situation may be for them *as a person.*

As the world changes with technological and scientific findings, organizations in sports are finding that the old way of handling their assets is not only outdated, but it's humanly wrong. While analytics has helped baseball people better understand the value of their players, science is helping them understand how sleep and rest, along with old staples such as nutrition and weight training, can help a player stay fresher over the course of a 162-game season. All of these findings are helping teams better understand how they can help their players develop as athletes and *as people.*

Talent Development and Distribution

The three most important areas of any organization are:

1. *Talent acquisition – recruit people*
2. *Talent development – develop people*
3. *Talent distribution – put people in a position to be successful*

In "Scouting and Drafting," we highlighted key aspects for talent acquisition. In this section, we'll expand on that and work through the other two points as well.

Player development is one craze of today's game. Between the springs of 2011 and 2018, the average size of a player-development staff among major league clubs increased 51 percent, from an average of 51 people in 2011 to 77 in 2018.

It's important to note that development *isn't* linear, and in baseball, it's also not just about the skills of how to play the game. When young players come to the Yankees, they are talented and hungry to find success. It's up to Kevin Reese, Senior Director of Player Development, to figure out the best ways to keep those players striving to be the best.

Development is so important to the Yankees that processes run through the two people with the most authority. Whatever Reese needs to be successful, he asks of general manager Brian Cashman, who goes directly to owner Hal Steinbrenner for funding.

Each season the Yankees employ roughly 300 prospects; of those, about 170 will make it to rookie ball and only 25 percent of that cut will make it to minor league A-ball. Overall, 10 percent of prospects will reach the majors for the Yankees.

For many players, talent has carried them this far, but baseball is a humbling sport, one in which an offensive player is considered Hall of Fame worthy if they get a hit three times every ten at-bats—or a 30 percent success rate. But being able to hit and throw a baseball is just one aspect of the sport.

Baseball players have lives outside of the ballpark. So, while it's important that a player learns to hit the off-speed pitch and master their footwork in the infield to cut down on errors, it's also critical that the athletes learn how to be contributing members of society. Just as college is supposed to prepare students for a long life ahead of them, the minor leagues present an opportunity to do the same with baseball players. If Reese's players drown in early failures, then he isn't doing his job in developing *all* aspects of his *people*.

One of the development processes for the younger Yankees involves learning how to conduct themselves as adults, as well as intensive training on American laws. When a high percentage of the player pool is of international origin, it is important to remember that laws, like development, aren't equal across the world. Customs and norms in Venezuela are different than in America.

The Yankees don't expect, for example, a Venezuelan-born player to immediately understand cultural differences, both major and subtle, when they first come to the organization. At their base in Tampa, the Yankees have police officers come in once a month to teach the international players what they can and cannot do in America and to help better explain laws that don't exist in their home countries. The players are taught the harsh consequences for actions that aren't aligned with their policies and the law, including jail time or even deportation.

It took Cashman time to figure out that what American-born players take for granted can be difficult for international players to learn, and from 2005 to 2014 those prospects were expected to learn on their own once they entered the Yankees' organization.

International players had to navigate matters such as how to apply for a social security card, get cash out of an ATM, or even how to order food. Reese was once quoted as saying that he knew guys who only knew enough English to order McDonald's. Some players came over to the United States and *had never even experienced electricity*.

The Yankees decided to make a change in their player handling when it became obvious that their international players struggled with what seemed like minor tasks. They now have academies in many of the countries that they select from each year, and they employ twenty-five part and full-time teachers with the goals to hone baseball skills, fill out body frames with food, and educate the players to at least a sixth-grade level before they come to the United States.

Since 2014, other significant player-development improvements have come from various front-office Yankee executives. For example, Steinbrenner hired nutritionists to teach the players how to purchase food and cook for themselves. Reese hired teachers to help the players learn English, so that when they eventually got to New York they could do interviews in the language.

One of the methods for teaching the prospects English is to have them watch the former hit sitcom, *Friends*, whose actors and actresses talk slowly, enunciate clearly, and speak the type of English that isn't heard in the Bronx. Interestingly enough, by watching *Friends*, the players also learn values and lessons in life, such as maintaining friendships through hardship or how to recover from heartbreak and adversity.

The Yankees were the first to interview their amateur players before selecting them in the draft. This process began because of internal questions regarding a person who would later make a significant impact on playoff teams, but before that, had trouble dodging perceptions regarding his large physical stature.

Kendall Carter, a national crosschecker scout for the Yankees, discovered Aaron Judge while Judge was still playing college ball at California State University, Fresno. Judge is listed as six feet, seven inches and 282 pounds. Twelve players in baseball history have been six foot six inches or taller and had more than one thousand plate appearances—and only one, former Yankee Dave Winfield, is in the Hall of Fame.

In 2005, the Yankees lured Chad Bohling away from the National Football League's (NFL) Jacksonville Jaguars, and made him their director of mental conditioning. Because players of Judge's height had a limited record of success, the Yankees wanted to be certain that his mental makeup was as strong as his physical size before selecting him with a precious draft pick. It was Bohling who interviewed and cleared Judge as fit for New York.

Bohling is part of the vetting process for all amateur players, with the hope that prospects without the proper makeup will be weeded out before they ever put on Yankee pinstripes. When it comes to established veterans, the process can be simpler. For example, the Yankees can look at a player's success in higher-leverage games, such as postseason play. But even this approach isn't surefire; the Yankees traded for Oakland Athletics' ace Sonny Gray prior to the 2017 trade deadline, largely based on the fact that the pitcher was an All-Star and had pitched well enough as a twenty-three-year-old in 2013—his only playoff appearance with the Athletics.

Gray was under contractual control for two more seasons, and it seemed like he would be the long-term anchor the Yankees had been seeking to solidify their starting rotation. But after a mediocre ending to 2017, Gray struggled mightily in 2018. He also had difficulties with the daily pressures of New York and the media.

By the time the 2019 season started, Gray was in a different city (Cincinnati) and wearing a different uniform, far away from the daily burden of the concrete jungle. Gray serves as a cautionary tale against small sample sizes, and how even established players don't follow linear paths to development.

Back in 2017, the Yankees created the "Captain's Camp." The masterclass is a four-week crash course on leadership for younger Yankees, and in the past it has been hosted by former greats such as Derek Jeter, Andy Pettitte, and Jorge Posada. Pettitte, who was hired in 2019 by the Yankees as a special advisor to Brian Cashman, told one group of budding Yankees how he dealt with adversity and the importance of preparation, and he also shared tips on how to handle the mental aspects of the game.

Judge once went through a Captain's Camp and said, "We get to talk to a lot of old veterans and older scouts and a lot of our staff members about how they handle themselves on and off the field, how they respected the game, how they played the game.

"That's great," Judge continued. "A lot of guys don't get the opportunity to hear from a lot of the great players like we have."

According to *Baseball America*, the Yankees have had fifty-five different top-thirty prospects reach the big leagues since 2007, ten more than any other club, and they lead baseball in pitching Wins Above Replacement (WAR) from the farm system at +119.6 WAR, with the Dodgers a distant second at +96.7 WAR.[50] Prior to the start of the 2019 season, the Yankees led baseball in WAR, produced by homegrown players since 2007.

1. *Yankees: +193.2 WAR*
2. *Diamondbacks: +191.6 WAR*
3. *Red Sox: +191.0 WAR*
4. *Reds: +176.0 WAR*
5. *Rockies: +170.3 WAR*

Even with all of the player-development improvements, playing the game of baseball is still unbelievably hard. The Yankees have invested heavily in cognitive and social development to improve the

---

[50] A number used to summarize a player's total contributions to their team in one statistic.

slim chances of their players advancing all the way to the major leagues. The Yankees' scouting game is one of the strongest in baseball, and they sign kids of good character.

Their selection and development are not perfect science, and may never be, but by putting their faith in their *people*, the Yankees' development programs continue to produce big-league-ready players through their own efforts, without having to rely so heavily on outside reinforcements.

Have a Growth Mindset

Brian Cashman's growth philosophy is simple: "Development involves patience." The old Yankee regimes ate patience for lunch; now it's a foundational pillar for all business-related decisions.

Development also isn't exclusive to amateur players scouted and drafted by the Yankees. Proof of this is the success story of the former dynamic Yankees shortstop, Didi Gregorius.

Gregorius is as charismatic as they come: He's well-liked in the world of baseball, and he plays the game with the enthusiasm of a kid, which particularly endeared him to Yankee fans. Whether he was posting an emoji-filled tweet crediting his Yankee teammates for the latest victory or flashing emoji selfie sticks in the Yankees' dugout, Gregorius's presence was one of the most important aspects of the Yankees' good-person and fun culture. But however important Gregorius was to the Yankees, there was a period when it wasn't even certain that he could produce enough to get consistent playing time.

Gregorius made his debut in 2012 with the Cincinnati Reds, before he was traded that off-season to the Arizona Diamondbacks. During two seasons in the desert, Gregorius never played more than 103 games, and his batting average dropped to a pedestrian .226 in 2014. Gregorius's stellar defense was a primary reason he got to play as often as he did with the Diamondbacks, not his ability to hit.

During the 2014–15 off-season, Cashman saw Gregorius as a player who could significantly improve the Yankees' defense at shortstop. Acquiring Gregorius also meant they'd be getting a player who was young and cost-controlled, but had yet to reach his potential.

Cashman had been taught by the likes of former GM Gene Michael that championship teams had a "strong spine" up the middle, meaning at catcher, second base, center field, and of course, shortstop. Cashman was seeking a replacement for the retired captain, Derek Jeter, and at the very least Gregorius would provide better defense than the aging Jeter did during his final injury-ridden seasons.

It was a gamble, to be sure, but Cashman traded for Gregorius anyway. At the start of the 2015 season, Gregorius was the only Yankees starter under the age of thirty. The Yankees knew they didn't have a clubhouse or a defensive problem with Gregorius, but if they could figure out his hitting enough to make him even an average batter, they were going to be thrilled with the investment.

Before coming to the Yankees, Gregorius's biggest weakness was his inability to learn from his failures at the plate. The Yankees analytics department found video showing pitchers throwing Gregorius fewer balls in the strike zone than most players, hoping he would chase. The Yankees wanted Gregorius to stop chasing fastballs up and away, and they believed that by laying off these pitches, Gregorius could draw more walks *and* increase his power numbers at the plate.

Gregorius, to his credit, once he was shown the video evidence, became more eager than ever to learn and listen to the analytics behind his game. Since 2015, he increased his home run production from nine that season to a career-high twenty-seven in 2018, while that same season drawing a career-high forty-eight walks, which was almost double that of his previous career best.

Gregorius is a true success story for development. Replacing a Yankees legend and former captain can be a daunting task, but Gregorius handled the demands and pressures of the post-Derek Jeter era with a class that his predecessor would surely approve of, and Gregorius became a star and clubhouse leader in his own right.

"A lot of times, guys put a label on a person without letting the person develop," Gregorius said of his own progress. "There's always people that are going to doubt you. At the end, it's up to you how hard you want to work."

Dealing with External Pressure

Development is physical, mental, and skills-based. In New York, it's also learning to deal with the pressures of the New York media—which creates a unique situation for the Yankees. When Giancarlo Stanton was traded to the Yankees prior to the 2018 season, one of the first elements he noticed was that in Miami (where he previously played for the Marlins) there were three beat writers, and in New York he counted roughly fifty members of the press. Whether someone's an executive, manager, coach, or player, the toughest part of the job is dealing with the press, and it gets harder each year because of the instantaneous cycle in which people expect to get news.

Two people who understand the demands of the New York media better than most are former managers Joe Torre and Joe Girardi. "I didn't realize it when I first got to New York," Torre once said. "But after having been there a little bit I understood that playing in New York was unlike playing in any other place. People either really embraced it, or they just had a problem with it."

Torre's successor as manager, Girardi, echoed that sentiment, saying, "People [Yankees fans] are so emotional and intense."

Girardi's understanding of the New York media from his playing and coaching days with the Yankees surely helped him as manager. His ability to emphasize to his players not to panic over the course of a long season was instrumental in keeping a cohesive clubhouse.

"I think you have to be careful," Girardi said, "that when you lose a couple days in a row or three in a row, you don't push a panic button."

Having that mentality is important for the Yankees players, especially the inexperienced ones. They are all under a microscope each day with the media, and learning how to deal with their presence can go a long way toward being able to perform to the best of their abilities, day in and day out.

Enter Jason Zillo.

Each spring, the Yankees' vice president of communication and media relations runs a seminar with the youngest players to prepare them for the New York media blitz. Zillo has been in his role since 2007, and his primary responsibility is to help shape the perception of the Yankees' brand. As Cashman's right-hand man, Zillo creates many of the development programs and policies the Yankees' players go through before getting to the Bronx.

"Cash and I have a lot of dialogue," Zillo says of their relationship. "He wants to know what I'm picking up on with the young guys I'm interacting with every day, and we're putting them through the media training program at a young age."

The Yankees try to pull out all the stops when it comes to their players dealing with the media. One example is they stage role-play workshops for players with less than four years of service time. The purpose of the training is for the entire team to have *one voice.*

The Yankees want all of their players to handle issues and topics in a single manner to eliminate as many chances as possible for unnecessary distraction inside the clubhouse. The players are taught how to handle questions in regard to everything and anything from poor play, to world catastrophes, to what they did out on the town during the previous night.

If the New York media can be a burden, the Yankees do their best to ensure their players are appropriately prepared to handle it. With this version of the Yankees, there is no sparring with other players, coaches, managers, or executives through an external source. This adaptation of the Yankees gives the media the answers they need to write their stories and then move on with their day.

Zillo and Cashman have created "good clubhouse guys" who are fully capable of dealing with external pressure, and have seen their efforts snowball into a dynamic that players on the Yankees appreciate and players from other organizations envy.

Summary of *Development Isn't Always Linear*

The *Culture of Excellence* continues to thrive in New York as a result of *patience* and a willingness to truly develop their *people*. It's a process that's years in the making, and it's a practice that has paid dividends for the franchise—development allows the team to streamline all of its other baseball efforts.

Talent development and distribution help bridge the full growth of a player. It's one matter to find great talent, it's another to be able to help them grow and thrive within a system. Most organizations fail at the latter, and that's what leads to turnover, toxic cultures, and bad reputations.

Investing time and resources toward individual growth leads to more happiness. That can be a major differentiating factor for a prospect and their long-term fulfillment. But it's crucial to understand that development happens at different speeds for different people. If we put everyone on one path, then we may lose out on the fruit of our labor.

Understanding each person and their strengths, challenges, and goals will aid in building a learning process that is conducive for the masses, and not just for the elite.

Chapter Nine

Moneyball, Sabermetrics, and Analytics

M ajor League Baseball has existed for over 150 years. The least surprising fact in this book is that money has always been a central part of the conversation of the game.

The current baseball landscape is comprised in a way that is more complex than ever before. For its first century in existence, big-league players were bound to one team for life—an infamous title called "the reserve clause"—and were afforded a yearly salary, which is what *most* people in the current American business world are used to. In many states across the nation, when an individual signs an offer letter with an employer, that person broadly enters into "at-will employment," which means an at-will employee can be terminated at any moment for any legal reason.

Today's average American worker is treated similarly to baseball players prior to the establishment of the Major League Baseball Players Association (MLBPA). Baseball players *used to be* bound to a club to provide their services, essentially until it no longer suited them.

After multiple attempts to represent themselves failed, the current version of the MLBPA was established in 1953; however, it was not formally recognized as a union until 1966.[51] Given the dicey situation the MLBPA had been thrust into, Marvin Miller, named union leader after successfully leading the United Steelworkers, decided to focus on two primary factors for the players: an increase in their salary and the pledge to create a pension.

In the early stages of development, Miller's wisest foresight was to involve the players in the labor process. He wanted major leaguers to understand that the owners would *never* tell them about certain unalienable rights. As a way to break their obedience with owners, Miller would constantly tell them, "*You* are the game. Without you there is no game."

In 1967, the average salary for a player was a pedestrian $19,000, and salaries only amounted to 25 percent of revenue by the early 1970s. Surely there was ample opportunity for the players to leverage themselves as true assets, not ones who could be cut or traded at the will of their employer and without consent.

While the game of baseball grew, the players wanted to ensure there was a more accountable process between the money they were being given and the revenue teams made. Miller's eager students were quickly gaining knowledge, and as the players became more educated, the game changed dramatically, becoming more sophisticated and complex.

It was a process worth enduring for the players' sake. While negotiating original free agency terms,[52] Miller and the players tinkered with different models, but kept coming back to the number six being the year in which they felt they should be eligible to decide their baseball future without restrictions. Their own research had shown them that most players fell off and were out of the major leagues by year three, but if a player reached year six, then their chances of getting to ten were much higher *and* they could hit free

---

[51] As a humorous anecdote, the union wasn't even universally wanted or accepted by the ballplayers of the day, and it was even more vehemently opposed by the baseball owners.

[52] The baseball term used to describe an open market of ballplayers.

agency two times in a career: once at year six and again at year twelve.

Free agency was about to revolutionize the game forever.

The story of the economic revolution in baseball is important because it underscores the value that today's players have to their teams. Much of that story is known for the blood, sweat, and tears that resulted from the harsh negotiations that the players and the owners went through on numerous occasions from the time of Miller's appointment in 1966 until the disastrous 1994 strike, which wiped out almost two months of that year's regular season, plus the playoffs, and finally, the World Series altogether.

When all the fighting was done and the dust had settled, free agency *was* a game-changer for the sport. By 1995, the average salary for a baseball player was just a touch under $1.2 million, well above the $19,000 threshold the sport had seen only twenty-eight years earlier.

Moneyball

At the beginning of the Yankees' most recent dynasty, free agency was still the normal practice for most ball clubs to fill out their roster, but by the turn of the millennium, baseball was headed toward a whole new revolution: moneyball. The latest economic transformation changed the entire sport's landscape and forced its greatest organization to reinvent, before they once again faded into irrelevance.

All decisions have consequences, whether they are intended or not. That's the reality of life. The MLBPA pushed the boundaries of what was long considered "normal" when it came to money in the sport. Television deals, which rose 1,742 percent from 1971 to 1990, and stadium deals gave owners new lifeblood, in addition to traditional gate sales revenue, but because of the terms of the collective bargaining agreements (CBA), this also meant that more money needed to be distributed to the players.

Had all teams been created equal, there may not have been any issues at stake prior to the season-ending strike in 1994, but the disparity between the large and smaller market clubs was becoming bigger than ever before. Widely different television and stadium deals resulted in ten teams sliding into the red in 1991. Even after the strike, the Yankees generated $244 million in revenue in 2001, which still amounted to more than the combined income of the Montreal Expos, Minnesota Twins, Florida Marlins, and Kansas City Royals.

It was clear that competitive balance was becoming more of a serious issue within the sport. In most other industries, increased market share goes to the strongest companies. But baseball is a sport without a salary cap. In order to bring the game to more fans and put more "companies" in more cities, it was crucial that baseball alter its CBA to include revenue sharing among all the teams.

In 2001, MLB established a revenue-sharing system that is still largely in place today. At the time of implementation, the payroll ratio between the seven richest and seven poorest teams in baseball was 4:1. For comparison's sake, in the NBA it was 1.75:1, and in the NFL—both sports with salary caps in place—it was 1.5:1.

Prior to 2000, local income had been the *only* source of revenue. This included stadium and television deals, as well as the number of tickets sold each season. To boost national revenue, baseball created MLB Advanced Media in 2000, which handled the sports digital assets, and MLB.com launched in 2001. By 2018, each club received $118 million from local revenue sharing and $91 million apiece in national revenue sharing.

Since 2001, there has not been a single repeat champion in baseball, and there have been many teams that have ended long droughts en route to a championship: Boston Red Sox, 2004, first since 1918; Chicago White Sox, 2005, first since 1917; San Francisco Giants, 2010, first since 1954; Chicago Cubs, 2016, first since 1908.

In addition, four franchises captured their first-ever World Series title: Arizona Diamondbacks (2001), Anaheim Angels (2002), Houston Astros (2017), and Washington Nationals (2019).

Revenue sharing has done what baseball set it out to do: create a more *competitive balance.*

Moneyball is a term that has been glorified by Hollywood and Brad Pitt, but simply defined, it means to look for market inefficiencies. Prior to the movie, *Moneyball* was a best-selling book by Michael Lewis, and prior to that it was *just an idea* that was percolating in the brain of Oakland Athletics' general manager Billy Beane.

How can teams find players who are undervalued and not overpay for overvalued ones?

In a copycat league, that idea was then taken and applied by all (or most) of the other teams in baseball, and although there have been various amounts of success, there is no denying the lasting impact the term has had on the sport in regard to the way executives view and evaluate players.

Like most businesses, baseball used to operate much more on trust and intuition than it did on data and analytics. In its current version, baseball is an industry that absolutely cannot afford to rely on pure *guts,* much to the dismay of the old-schoolers out there. Forbes reported that Major League Baseball recorded a revenue of $10.3 billion in 2018. Luckily, because of technology and data, almost every part of the process of assembling a baseball team—scouting, drafting, free agency, arbitration—can be captured in ways past generations couldn't have imagined.

With more clubs gaining skill in identifying the value of talent, more teams theoretically have a better chance of competing and winning. But Beane's concept of moneyball was hardly revolutionary in some of its basic elements.

Beane wanted the Athletics to run more like a traditional business than he wanted it to run like a baseball team. This concept started with role responsibilities. Beane told the *Boston Herald* in 2003, "We're [the front office] going to run the organization from the top down. We're controlling player personnel. That's our job. I don't apologize for that. There's this belief that a baseball team starts with the manager first. It doesn't."

Beane's statement brought to light the long-held assumption that the manager was responsible for building a ball club. Even in the old days, this idea was more fantasy than reality. Rarely was the manager the one compiling the roster of a ball club.

Managers *were* always the glue guys, the culture police before culture became a concept, and their value in terms of an everyday visible presence was undeniable. In the past, they also had more of a say in decisions regarding on-field play. Managers were the ones making the call to the bullpen to replace a weary starting pitcher; they were the ones choosing to pinch hit with a short bench late in a tight game; they were in charge of just about all in-game strategy with a group of players given to them by the front office.

Billy Beane fundamentally changed the way the manager and front-office relationships worked, and since the outset of moneyball, managers have seen their on-field role altered dramatically to resemble more of a figurehead in the dugout than that of an actual in-game tactician.

Need proof?

Prior to the 2018 season, four new managers were hired who hadn't had *any* prior managerial experience at any level in baseball. One of those first-time managers, Boston's Alex Cora, led the 2018 Red Sox to the franchise's fourth World Series title of the millennium and their first championship since 2013.

While some of the moneyball concepts were simple to implement, other conditions of Beane's model required more innovation. In order to change, people of influence in baseball would have to buy into the power of technology. Scouting reports and statistics generated by computers led to many revolutions in the sport, like Wins Above Replacement—a sabermetric statistic developed to sum up a player's total contributions—launch angle, and spin rates.

One of the most dramatic changes is the way offense has come to be viewed. In the past, there was too much value in batting averages and stolen bases, while there wasn't enough value placed on walks and extra-base hits. On-base plus slugging (OPS)—a new statistic calculated as the sum of a player's on-base percentage and slugging average—was created to showcase the ability of a player both to get on base and hit for power, two of the most important offensive skills.

Plate discipline also became a desired trait, as analytics showed on-base percentage and seeing a high number of pitches per plate appearance equaled a higher value to the offense. Strikeouts on offense were the equivalent of simple math: They were the most expensive out a hitter could make, because the ball wasn't put in play; thus, the opportunity to reach base in any way was rendered dead.

Analytics proved that by trying to manipulate games with low-percentage moves, teams were scoring fewer runs than they should have. Without runs being scored, it's tough to win a ball game. Thus, analytics showed bunts, stolen bases, and hit-and-runs all contributed to unnecessary outs and were extremely self-defeating.

The money that goes to individual players has affected how the roster of a ball club is evaluated. It made it so that each team was now doing everything possible to minimize risk, because they couldn't afford to have a player not work out. If money wasn't being spent on the right players, then it no longer mattered how much money a team had.

As the baseball landscape changed to become a multibillion-dollar business, the game was able to attract well-educated minds and more non-baseball people to build robust systems. The sport was becoming more of a science and more of a *business* than ever before.

How Have Moneyball and Analytics Affected the Yankees?

The Yankees, of course, had once been a primary beneficiary of the old system. Prior to revenue sharing and the first wave of analytics, it wasn't imperative to their yearly success (although it sure helped) to have a minor league system stocked with top prospects. If the Yankees needed reinforcements along the way, they would trade their best minor league assets and throw in cash to get a proven commodity. Money used to be of no burden to George Steinbrenner or to the old CBA regulations.

Season after season during the dynasty years, the Yankees pulled off a trade to bolster their postseason run, like first baseman Cecil Fielder in 1996 and designated hitter David Justice in 2000, who were two huge midseason acquisitions, and both players made major contributions toward eventual World Series titles. If it wasn't a midseason trade, then it was an off-season one, like acquiring second baseman Chuck Knoblauch in 1998 and pitcher Roger Clemens in 1999.

Signing major-league free agents outright for any price was a luxury only a few teams could afford, but none like the Yankees, who throughout the 1990s and early 2000s signed names such as former Cy Young Award winner, David Cone and rival divisional foe and pitching ace, Mike Mussina.

During that time, the Yankees used to have so much more money than other teams that they could acquire big-name stars *and* they could afford to keep their core intact by re-signing their own players. Bernie Williams, one of the Yankees' biggest stars, reached free agency after the 1998 season and was brought back for $87.5 million. Cone, Scott Brosius, Joe Girardi, and Paul O'Neill all reached free agency at one point during the dynasty years, and the Yankees were able to retain their services, fending off other suitors in the process.

But in what could be considered a preview of the future model, core young stars like Derek Jeter, Mariano Rivera, Jorge Posada, and Andy Pettitte were all earning less than $1 million per season during and through a chunk of the early dynasty years. So, while there was no luxury tax and no penalty for spending over a certain amount, a large part of the Yankees' success came from the fact that their younger prospects had developed into serviceable stars. This allowed the Yankees to supplement holes with proven players from other clubs by trading assets or giving away large gobs of money.

The Yankees' past methodology in roster building was *see hole, fill hole*. There was not sufficient concern for efficiency of resources or flipping older players to set up for the future. But the modern game makes it so that free-agent spending sprees are like fad diets: The short-term results may be good, but you often end up in worse shape. The draft is the path to sustainable success—it's the eat-well-and-exercise approach to team-building.

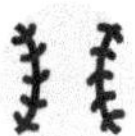

How did moneyball change the way the Yankees operate? The addition of national revenue was, in itself, a great deal of foresight for MLB and led to poorer clubs being able to make bigger investments to their young stars. This postponed their free agency and led to "team friendly" deals becoming the norm, not the exception.

Also, because of the moneyball movement, baseball front offices became savvier in their overall approach to player development. As a result, younger and less expensive players have not only been thrust into major league lineups, but they have performed at a higher rate than any generation before them. This has caused "older" players, especially those on the other side of "prime," (thirty-one or thirty-two years old) to find themselves *not* receiving large free-agent deals generations before them were accustomed to. Some players even found themselves out of work altogether.

The game has completely changed course from what used to have teams saddled with older veterans mixed in with select rookies and younger players. To compete in today's baseball means to get younger and stay young.

Immediately after the dynasty collapsed and the luxury tax was put in place, the Yankees' brass decided to use their financial might to prove that nothing could stop them from winning championships. By 2004, it had been *three whole seasons* without a title in New York, and the Boss, feeling his internal time clock ticking faster and faster, was desperate for another ring and reverting to old habits.

The George Steinbrenner-led organizational policy did not take into account what it meant to spend over the threshold of the luxury tax (the current "soft salary cap" in baseball), which assessed teams at a rate of 17.5 percent and escalated rates for repeat offenders. The luxury tax was contributing to a slow and painful death for the Yankees.

After acquiring Alex Rodriguez prior to the 2004 season, the Yankees had four players with contracts of $100 million or more.[53] They quickly became the number one repeat offender for escalating penalty rates. In all, prior to the 2018 season, the Yankees had paid out $340 million to other ball clubs. Steinbrenner and many Yankees executives took too long to realize the significance of their supplementing the rest of the league and even their own divisional rivals.

In 2007, the Red Sox won their second World Series title in four seasons, and in 2008 the Tampa Bay Rays reached the World Series before losing to the Philadelphia Phillies. The Yankees, meanwhile, finished second in the American League East in 2007, for the first time since 1997. The 2008 season saw the Yankees completely out of the playoffs for the first time since before the strike-shortened campaign of 1994.

As reality began to set in, it became clear that the Yankees could no longer just use their money to fix their problems. But they certainly tried. After teams locked up their young stars before they hit

---

[53] Joining Kevin Brown, Derek Jeter, and Jason Giambi.

free agency,[54] the Yankees were tasked with trying to find value in veteran players who were once stars but had seen better days on the playing field.[55]

During this time, less regard was paid toward cultural fit, and the players the Yankees brought in created headaches and drama within the clubhouse that had rarely been experienced during the dynasty years. And while most of the players did make *some* contribution to teams that still won a lot of regular-season games, they did not have the same poise in the postseason as players during the dynasty did. As a result, many of them struggled further to fit into New York amid the increasing pressure and burden of replacing the old guard and starting a new dynasty.

The trades that the Yankees executed during that time period also left their minor league system bare. There were no Jeters, Riveras, or Pettittes coming through the system, because they were all being traded for veteran players. Minor league pitching prospects were being rushed to the majors, and GM Brian Cashman and his front office were hoarding mediocre prospects, deeming them untouchable.

During the dynasty years, pitching was key to the team's dominance, but from 1990 (Andy Pettitte) to 2004 (Phil Hughes) the Yankees drafted 397 pitchers, none of whom made significant contributions at the major league level.

When they did have some form of contribution from a pitcher, the Yankees dealt the player away before they could make more of an impact. Just ask Ted Lilly, who was twenty-six in 2002 when he was traded for Jeff Weaver—a reliable arm for the Detroit Tigers but a player who had a known fragile personality. Weaver's stint in the

---

[54] Like the Blue Jays (Roy Halladay and Chris Carpenter), Indians (Grady Sizemore), Milwaukee Brewers (Ben Sheets), Houston Astros (Roy Oswalt), and the Minnesota Twins (Johan Santana).

[55] Jaret Wright, Carl Pavano, Kevin Brown, Randy Johnson, Gary Sheffield, Raúl Mondesí, Javier Vázquez, Kenny Lofton, and Kei Igawa headline a brutal laundry list of players who came to the Yankees via either free agency or trade between 2002 and 2007.

Bronx was, predictably, short and uninspiring. He gave up the winning home run in Game 4 of the 2003 World Series and was run out of the Bronx two months later. Lilly, meanwhile, became an All-Star in 2004 and compiled a career WAR almost fifteen points higher than Weaver.

Compounding matters was the organization's inability to take advantage of low-hanging fruit. By 2004, Carlos Beltrán had been the 1999 Rookie of the Year, finished in the top ten in Most Valuable Player voting once, and was a two-time All-Star selection. Oh, and he had just completed a monster postseason run with the Houston Astros, hitting over .400 while smashing eight home runs.

Beltrán, still only twenty-seven years old at the time, was a free agent and willing to take a 20 percent discount to play for the Yankees. Instead, the Yankees used the money they could have given to Beltrán to try and shore up their pitching, going on a twenty-two-day spending spree that saw them add three pitchers well past their prime years—all of whom made little to no major contributions during their time in New York.

As the baseball landscape changed, the Yankees found it increasingly difficult to supplement their roster with young and versatile talent. Instead, they wound up with players like Jason Giambi—a slugger, but one who took himself out of a game in the only World Series he ever played, because of a "bad knee," when in reality it was because Giambi had difficulty throwing the ball from first to second base. Giambi would rather save himself embarrassment than fight to win a *World Series* game.

Older players also meant being more prone to injury. In the same game that Giambi took himself out of the lineup, pitcher David Wells removed himself from his Game 5 start after throwing a one-two-three first inning, telling manager Joe Torre, "I can't go." Only twenty-four hours earlier, Wells was bragging at a news conference about the lack of conditioning he needed to succeed.

The "quick fix approach" being used by the Yankees from the end of the dynasty through the 2008 season had little regard for the role *character* played to fit into New York and the Yankees' clubhouse. If they were ever going to rid themselves of the vile cycle they were in, the organization needed to improve their ability to discover, obtain, and develop elite talent.

After the 2008 season, a year with no playoff baseball, the Yankees got a temporary reprieve. After multiple bad contracts came off the books following that season, the Yankees had money to spend, with a core in Jeter, Pettitte, Posada, and Rivera, who were eager to win their fifth ring together. They also finally had a few younger players like Robinson Canó and Phil Hughes, who were contributing to the big-league squad.

The perfect storm of circumstances led to the off-season free-agent additions of CC Sabathia, AJ Burnett, and Mark Teixeira. With the "Core Four" having career seasons in 2009 and Brian Cashman bringing in the reinforcements, the Yankees won their twenty-seventh World Series title. But even the Yankees had to have known the quick-fix formula would lead to a fiasco further up the road.

It didn't take long for the disaster to set in. The Yankees never won another championship after 2009, and by 2013 they were in the same position they had been immediately after the dynasty. The team was old, they were expensive, and they were bleeding money to everyone else in baseball.

Other clubs were lapping the Yankees in their understanding of the consequences of the new CBA and revenue sharing. It was time to reinvent themselves again, or it would soon look like 1985 in the Bronx.

Using Data and Information, Part II: Gaining a Competitive Edge

Numbers and stats have always been important, especially to the history of the game of baseball, but it's never been more important to compile quantitative data that front offices, managers, coaches, *and* players all buy into to support decision-making processes. Part of building a championship-caliber formula starts with analytics, and with a staff of fifteen as of 2017, the Yankees' group is the largest in all of baseball.

Leaving no stone unturned, each spring the Yankees assign an iPad Pro to each player and email daily updates of individual and team analysis. It's a simple concept but one that is appreciated, particularly by the players[56]—most of whom now come up to the big leagues with data being a central part of their baseball experience.

Since all GMs want their teams to get cheaper and younger, the most valuable commodity in today's game is the cost-controlled player at a minimum salary who can also produce at the big-league level. Basic science tells us that once players hit thirty-one or thirty-two years old, performance begins to depreciate due to age plus wear and tear on the body. For a team to be successful, they have to draft and develop players who can complement the veterans *and* be cornerstone contributors to the roster.

Since 1965, MLB has required all amateurs to enter the league through a yearly draft, where selection is determined by the reverse order of the team's previous year's finish in the standings. In the current system, the club that drafts and signs a player holds their rights for the first seven years in the minors and first six years in the majors, while all players become salary arbitration-eligible after year three in the big leagues. Additionally, players with at least ten years of service who have spent the past five consecutive seasons with the same team, earn "Ten-and-Five" rights. Under these circumstances, ten-and-five rights function as a full no-trade clause for the player.

These rules and regulations help us better understand the guidelines the Yankees must use in order to comply with the current CBA. Like most businesses, baseball is cyclical; bad teams get dibs on the best prospects in the draft, veterans age out and sometimes create

---

[56] Yankees first baseman, Luke Voit, has spoken about the differences between the St. Louis Cardinals and Yankees in terms of analytics, stating that the increased knowledge—and access to it—has been a major factor in his consistent on-field contributions since being traded to New York in 2018.

salary constraints, and either a club locks up a homegrown stud to an early extension or they hit the open market once eligible.

Grasping what can help now *and* in the future is paramount for long-term success. As the league trends toward more competitive parity, the window to vie for a championship gets smaller. Whereas in the 1990s it could have been attributed to steroids, today's increasing level of play has resulted from *information*. Simply put, it's harder than ever to put a sustainable product on the field in today's baseball world, but with increased fiscal responsibility, the Yankees have the opportunity to continue contending far into the future.

An Outlook: The Competitive Baseball Landscape

For all of the competitive balance throughout MLB, life in the Yankees' division—the American League East—as it is currently constituted will never be easy to navigate. The other teams in their division, including Toronto, Baltimore, and Boston, all have large payrolls *and* the ability to develop more revenue at a higher clip than most teams in baseball. All three franchises can claim to have a great ballpark experience and they have all had recent winning pedigree.

The Toronto Blue Jays won back-to-back World Series titles in 1992 and 1993—just as the Yankees' *Culture of Excellence* was first being formed. But the 1994 strike badly altered the fate of the franchise and tipped the balance to be more in favor of New York and Boston. After a long run of dreadful baseball, the Blue Jays made it to the American League Championship Series in 2015 and 2016. The organization is once again in a strong position moving forward, having shed their big contracts, giving them plenty of payroll flexibility to pair with top prospects.

The Orioles have made the playoffs five different times since 1996. They, too, have payroll flexibility in the future to combine with up-and-coming prospects. The franchise has finally entered the analytical era after a long resistance with the previous regime, which included former Yankees manager, Buck Showalter, and should soon be fielding a more competitive team.

The Red Sox exist as the biggest continued threat to the Yankees. Their savviness with analytics and player development, matched with an ownership that is willing to spend and pay the luxury tax, make them an organization that can continually *reload* instead of going through a *rebuilding* period like most teams endure. Boston has defeated the Yankees in the playoffs the last two times they met, in 2004 and more recently in 2018. Both seasons ended with the Red Sox winning the World Series, and Boston has also captured two additional titles this millennium, in 2007 and 2013.

Building Depth

A long time ago, the Yankees figured out that not only do the best players command the highest compensation, but they will also deliver sustained and remarkable results. This is the rule, not the exception. However, there are plenty of instances in which lower paid players provide a higher on-field value than their more expensive counterparts do.

Brian Cashman and the front office are always doing their best to determine the most efficient route, but it's a fluid experience. For example, in 2019, the Yankees went into the season with their starting outfield set to be Giancarlo Stanton in left field, Aaron Hicks in center, and Aaron Judge in right, with Brett Gardner starting the season as the fourth outfielder. This setup came after Cashman decided against signing any large free-agent contracts during the 2018–19 off-season.

Injuries ravaged the Yankees' outfield during the 2019 season. First, before the season even began, Hicks was placed on the injured list (IL) with a lower back injury, then Stanton went down on April 1, and finally, Judge added to the injury woes in late April with an oblique strain.

Cashman's decision not to sign anyone during the off-season loomed larger each time a Yankee hit the IL. Thus, the GM was forced to purchase journeyman first-round draft pick Cameron Maybin from the Cleveland Indians and parse together the rest of the outfield with prospect Clint Frazier, who missed most of the 2018 season with concussion-like symptoms. Mike Tauchman was also acquired during spring training via trade with the Colorado Rockies after Hicks hit the IL. Then the Yankees were forced to play the thirty-five-year-old Gardner every day, when they had hoped to keep the longest-tenured Yankee fresher throughout the year by splitting up his time during the long season as the fourth (rotational) outfielder.

Cashman's faith in his system's depth proved worthy and wise as Frazier, Tauchman, and Maybin all put together surprising seasons with high levels of contribution, the chance for which only came about because of all the injuries. The combination of Frazier, Tauchman, and Maybin cost the Yankees just over the big-league minimum in combined salary, and the trio produced a combined WAR of 4.3, helping lead the Yankees to the playoffs.

Sometimes it *does* reward teams to *not* overpay players in free agency.

The Future of Data and Information

Market inefficiencies—or the moneyball concept—are increasingly harder to find in today's game of baseball because of the access to information. Ben Lindbergh and Sam Miller write of this point in their best-selling publication, *The Only Rule Is It Has To Work*, saying, "... As the unexploited advantages available to teams shrink, researchers sift for still smaller ones."

Spray charts of batted balls, heat maps of pitches thrown, and Statcast tracking of launch angle and spin rate—these are all examples of measures in the current game that fall under the wider umbrella of analytics.

The challenge with the data (outside the question of how much is considered an overload for players, managers, and executives) is that *anyone* can access most of it, and that makes finding an edge all the more difficult to achieve. If the Yankees are to continue their winning form, they will have to find ways to outmaneuver all of the teams in their division—including the Tampa Bay Rays, a low payroll franchise that adapts as well as any in the sport and uses analytics as a tool to keep pace with the financial giants of the game.

Players are more curious than ever. They want to learn, and there are fewer clubs that are unequipped to give them that information. The difference between moneyball and the current analytics movement is that moneyball was highly focused on finding market inefficiencies and less worried about how to develop players. The next phase of the data revolution is dedicated to making players better.

In another Lindbergh collaboration, *The MVP Machine*, he and fellow author Travis Sawchik write, "Teams have a stronger grasp than ever on what makes players valuable. Now they're zeroing in on how to turn non-prospects into prospects, middling major leaguers into MVP candidates, and less dramatically but on an ever more widespread scale, good big leaguers into *better* big leaguers."

What does a team do when they are trying to break a bad habit? For the Yankees, all they have to do is look at the accomplishments of the dynasty years: The franchise discovered the formula for sustainable excellence not so long ago. At the midpoint of the 2010s, Hal Steinbrenner and Brian Cashman decided they wanted to replicate the equation and return the Yankees to tenable dominance.

A practical, but profitable, approach toward business is the overarching game plan for the modern-day Yankees. In a landscape that has harsh ramifications for overspending, it's still crucial that the Yankees find a way to be bold enough to spend their money and improve their roster with other teams' players, as well as supplement it with their own "homegrown" players who are ready to make significant contributions in the major leagues.

Throughout the years, Cashman has made incremental adjustments to his scouting group and invested heavily in analytics to make safer bets on players. More of this smart handling of data and information is going to be needed to keep pace. After all, whether they will publicly say it or not, the other twenty-nine teams are *always* chasing the Yankees; if they somehow get ahead, they know that it won't be long until New York can make up the margin and even pull ahead. Being cognizant of the constant need to innovate *and* be smart with baseball-related decisions is the biggest factor for sustainable success in the future.

With their overall advantage in resources, the Yankees should always operate as a clean, efficient, and self-sustaining organization. The Yankees need to be a well-oiled machine—or *Death Star*, as Brian Cashman once referred to it—and should be able to function like a McDonald's, a brand that has processes so strong that someone can expect the same type of service and food quality in Japan as they do in America.

The ability to build a consistent winner and a title contender has never in baseball's history been harder, but the Yankees have the people in place and the resources to support them in their pursuit of continuing their *Culture of Excellence*.

Summary of *Moneyball, Sabermetrics, and Analytics*

Just as in scouting and drafting, the rest of the player evaluation process is currently more data-driven than at any point in baseball history. Information will continue to be a crucial aspect of roster building, but it's important to never lose sight of the human elements of player assessment.

There should be a balance, but that doesn't necessarily mean there's going to be harmony in the split. If analytics takes more weight than intuition, then so be it. But a team cannot solely rely on numbers in their decision-making process, just as there is evidence that they should not rely exclusively on instinct.

For the Yankees to continue their *Excellence*, they must continue to invest in and develop their analytic approach and relationships. They must remain financially cognizant of the harsh luxury tax consequences, but never forget the mighty wealth that sets them apart from their competitors. Smart with data *and* smart with money equates to a formula that we can all agree will lead to extended success and set a standard that all teams strive to meet.

KEY POINTS: PLAYER DEVELOPMENT AND ORGANIZATIONAL STRUCTURE

There are three main points of structure to player and organizational development:

- *Patience*
- *The human element*
- *Fiscal responsibility*

These marks allow for stability to set in, which is another great element of sustainable success. When an organization achieves long-term prosperity, it's easy to look back and point to one or more of these qualities as being contributing factors.

The Yankees' progress over the past thirty years has shown us how quickly the environment changes and how that has forced them to innovate many times since the early 1990s. Each time they've failed to keep up or understand the differing landscape, it has set them back further from their version of success.

So, while it may be nearly impossible to enact all the conditions on a yearly basis, the takeaway is that it's possible to recover during the tough times. That's when it's even more imperative to practice patience, the human element, and fiscal responsibility. The Yankees are Polaris, baseball's version of the North Star, and are a guiding light to help teams compete in times of failure *and* in times of triumph.

The Future of the Yankees and Creating Your *Culture of Excellence*

Winning isn't everything, but in baseball, being victorious sure helps from a morale standpoint and from a vantage of sustainability. For the Yankees, that goes a long way toward keeping everyone aligned with the vision, from both a cultural and a productivity perspective.

Check out these stats: During the Wild Card Era (1995–present), the Yankees have *eighteen seasons*—out of a possible thirty-four—of ninety or more triumphs; only the Atlanta Braves come close to sniffing that level of viability, with fifteen such seasons. In addition, during the Wild Card Era, the Yankees have won ninety-five games fifteen different times, and they are the only team in double digits.

By producing on a consistent basis, the Yankees have allowed for continuity to reign supreme even in the face of difficult transition cycles, like directly after the dynasty years or from the dead period of 2013–16. This is in stark contrast to the churn and burn approach of the franchise prior to the second suspension of George Steinbrenner.

The Yankees stand alone in cultural and organizational cohesion in a time period where the Boston Red Sox have dismissed five different general managers—also running through three managers in the same span—since former GM, Theo Epstein, packed his bags for Chicago in 2011. The Red Sox can reason with their decisions because they've won two more World Series crowns since Epstein skipped town. But they fired another GM during the 2019 season, and their most recent World Series winning manager was run out of town amid a sign-stealing scandal before the start of the 2020 season.

Have the Red Sox become a little *too* envious of the Yankees, and do they too closely resemble the Bronx Zoo from the 1980s? Only time will give us the answer, but some baseball people have gone so far as to compare current Red Sox owner John Henry to the late George Steinbrenner—brash and unwilling to accept defeat.

Regardless of the path Boston takes, there will be no knee-jerk reaction from the Yankees' side. Instead, the mandate in New York will remain regulated, with the patient and fiscally responsible approach that starts with Hal Steinbrenner and Brian Cashman and reverberates throughout the rest of the Yankees.

Final Points of Emphasis

Change in your organization *can* happen, but it *won't* happen overnight. More than anything, the story of the New York Yankees emphasizes how important it was for its top leader—George Steinbrenner—to evolve in order for the franchise to attain the success they were capable of. *Leadership starts at the highest point of an organization.* It's pretty simple: If Steinbrenner doesn't adjust his management style after his second suspension and during the early 1990s, the most recent Yankees dynasty never happens.

It's taken more than thirty years for one of the greatest franchises in the world to build a consistent and sustainable model for cultural excellence. It took this long because of the friction created by the resistance to change—first by the Boss, and later by Hal Steinbrenner—and because reaching for the mountaintop each year is *hard to do*.

Great leadership is a demanding role, and excellent cultures are laborious to uphold. But don't let that deter you from achieving your ambitions—if you've made it this far, I know that you'll succeed in building the team or company that you desire.

Remember, *change* can happen. It's just going to take *time*.

At the start of our journey, it was my sincere desire that you would interpret these stories about the Yankees and find aspects that resonate with you in your life. Baseball players are *people*, and baseball clubs are *businesses*, which means we *all* can relate to each, even if we don't work specifically in the industry or particularly enjoy the sport.

There are so many lessons, and it's possible that each time you read this book, depending on where you are in your career or in life, the information will gain a new or deeper meaning. That's the amazing part about stories: We can *always* be learning from them, and the education we gain from this book can sustain us now *and* be passed on to future generations.

I will leave you with an account of my personal favorites (with the pages they begin on noted for easy reference) and I challenge you to immediately incorporate them into your work or life.

You came here looking to create a *Culture of Excellence*; now go out there and do the work!

Colin's Favorites

- Steinbrenner's Leadership Profile, *page 7*
- Leading with Empathy, *page 9*
- Building Trust, *page 27*
- Establishing a Working Relationship with a Difficult Boss, *page 32*
- Displaying Accountability, *page 36*
- Being Unafraid to Have Difficult Conversations, *page 60*
- Emerging Leaders, *page 79*
- Being "Captain" Isn't the Only Requirement to Lead, *page 106*
- HOPE Week, *page 124*
- Have a Growth Mindset, *page 145*
- Using Data and Information, Part II: Gaining a Competitive Edge, *page 163*

Let the Talent 409 Leadership Academy Help You or Your Team Discover Your Talent Altitude!

At the Talent 409 Leadership Academy, we wholeheartedly believe that talent is not fixed. You can *always* grow and develop, just like the Yankees have over the course of the last thirty-plus years. But you have to be willing to do the work.

We consult and train many of the same competencies displayed throughout this book, in both corporate and sporting environments. Through our work we have seen countless people thrive in ways that, at one point, didn't seem possible.

If you or your team are looking to take that next step, please visit our site www.talent409.com where you can learn more about our solutions and schedule your FREE consultation.

Glossary of Sports Terms

All-Star: The league's best players, as voted by fans.

All-Star Game: An annual midseason matchup between the best players from the American and National Leagues.

America's Pastime: A nickname to describe the game of baseball.

American League (AL): Established in 1903, and one of two leagues that make up Major League Baseball.

American League (AL) East: Established in 1969, and now one of six divisions in baseball.

American League Division Series (ALDS): The second round of the playoffs.

American League Championship Series (ALCS): The third round of the playoffs.

Baby Bombers: The 2017 Yankees or minor league Yankees players.

Bang-bang play: A close play in baseball, usually involving a force out, in which the ball reaches a fielder's glove just before the runner's foot hits the base.

Batterymate: The catcher who is paired with a pitcher or the pitcher who is paired with a catcher.

Batting average: One of the oldest and most universal tools to measure a hitter's success at the plate.

Batting title: Given to the player with the highest batting average at the end of each season.

Boo Birds: The sound of disgust coming from a crowd at a sporting event after something they didn't like happens.

Biogenesis scandal: Broke in 2013 when players were accused of obtaining performance-enhancing drugs from the now-defunct clinic Biogenesis of America.

Blue-chip prospects: Players who have proven themselves to be among the best at their positions in their respective sports and are more sought after than others.

Bronx Zoo: A nickname given to the Yankees' teams of the mid-to-late 1970s.

Bunt: The batter loosely holds the bat in front of home plate and intentionally taps the ball into play.

Catcher: The catcher crouches directly behind home plate and is primarily responsible for receiving all of a pitcher's pitches.

Center fielder: The center fielder covers the middle portion of the outfield (when viewing the field from home plate).

Core Four: A nickname given to players on the mid-to-late 1990s Yankees' dynasty that includes Derek Jeter, Mariano Rivera, Andy Pettitte, and Jorge Posada.

Collective Bargaining Agreement (CBA): The agreement between the Major League Baseball Players Association and Major League Baseball describing the rules of employment and the financial structure of the game.

Cy Young Award: Given annually to the best pitchers in Major League Baseball, one each for the American League and National League.

Designated hitter (DH): A player who bats in place of the pitcher.

Earned run average (ERA): The number of earned runs a pitcher allows per nine innings.

Extra-base hit: Any hit that is not a single, meaning doubles, triples, and home runs.

Fall Classic: A nickname for the World Series, played each October to determine the champion of baseball.

First baseman: The first baseman positions himself to the right of the first base bag and toward the back of the infield dirt when no runner occupies first base or on the first base bag after a batter reaches first base.

Free agency: Players become free agents upon reaching six years of service time or when they are released from their organization prior to reaching six years of service time. A free agent is eligible to sign with any club for any terms to which the two parties can agree.

Front office: Refers to owners, general managers, and other executives that run a professional baseball team.

Gold Glove Award: Given annually to the players judged to have exhibited superior individual fielding performances at each fielding position in both the National League and the American League.

General Manager (GM): In most organizations, the general manager has final say in roster decisions (e.g., trades, free-agent signings) and coaching/front-office personnel (e.g., hiring, firing, promotions, reassignments).

Hall of Fame: A museum committed to preserving the history of baseball and celebrating the legendary players, managers, umpires, and executives who have made the game a fan favorite for more than a century.

Hit-and-run: A strategy used on offense. With a runner on first base, the strategy calls for the runner to break toward second base with the pitch and for the batter to swing at the pitch, no matter where it is, in order to put the ball in play.

Hustle double: When a hitter runs hard out of the batter's box and turns a single into a double.

Infield: The inner part of the field of play.

Injured list (IL): Allows clubs to temporarily remove players from the active roster.

Left fielder: The left fielder covers the left portion of the outfield grass (when viewing the field from home plate).

Luxury tax: A penalty for clubs that exceed a predetermined payroll threshold.

Moneyball: A term used for finding value where other teams don't see it, or "market inefficiencies."

Monument Park: A museum located in Yankee Stadium containing a collection of monuments, plaques, and retired numbers honoring distinguished members of the Yankees.

Major League Baseball (MLB): A professional baseball organization and the oldest of the major professional sports leagues in the United States and Canada.

MLB Advanced Media: A limited partnership of the club owners of Major League Baseball that is the internet and interactive branch of the league.

MLB.com: The official website of Major League Baseball.
Major League Baseball Players Association (MLBPA): The collective bargaining representative for all current Major League Baseball players.
Most Valuable Player (MVP): An honor typically bestowed upon the best-performing players in the Major Leagues.
National Basketball Association (NBA): A men's professional basketball league in North America.
National Football League (NFL): A professional American football league.
NL: National League.
NLDS: National League Division Series.
NLCS: National League Championship Series.
On-base percentage: Refers to how frequently a batter reaches base per plate appearance.
Opening Day: The day when MLB begins the season.
On-base plus slugging (OPS): Adds on-base percentage and slugging percentage to get one number that unites the two. It's meant to combine how well a hitter can reach base with how well he can hit for average and for power.
Old Timer's Day (OTD): A celebration of the baseball-related accomplishments of the Yankees' former players who have retired.
Outfield: The area of the field of play further from the batter than the infield.
Pitcher: Stands on the pitching mound, which is located in the center of the infield and sixty feet, six inches away from home plate.
Playoffs/postseason: A competition played by the top competitors after the regular season to determine the league champion or a similar accolade.
Reserve clause: Part of a player contract which states that the rights to players were retained by the team upon the contract's expiration. Players under these contracts were not free to enter into another contract with another team.
Rookie: A first-year player.

Rookie of the Year Award: Given annually to two outstanding rookie players, one each for the American League and National League.

Right fielder: The right fielder covers the right portion of the outfield grass (when viewing the field from home plate).

R2C2: Podcast featuring Ryan Ruocco and CC Sabathia.

Salary arbitration: Players who have three or more years of Major League service but less than six years become eligible for salary arbitration if they do not already have a contract for the next season.

Second baseman: The second baseman positions himself between the first and second base bags (closer to second base), typically toward the back of the infield dirt.

Shortstop: The shortstop positions himself between the third baseman and the second base bag.

Stolen base: Occurs when a baserunner advances by taking a base to which he isn't entitled.

Strikeout: Occurs when a pitcher throws any combination of three swinging or looking strikes to a hitter.

Subway Series: Rivalry games played between the two teams based in New York City, the Yankees and the Mets.

Super-utility: A versatile player who can play a multitude of positions.

The House That George Built: A nickname given to the current-day Yankee Stadium, representing the importance of George Steinbrenner.

The House That Ruth Built: A nickname given to the old Yankee Stadium, representing the importance of Babe Ruth.

Third baseman: The third baseman positions himself in the vicinity of the third base bag, facing home plate with the base in front of him and to the right.

Tommy John surgery: A procedure in which a partial or fully torn ulnar collateral ligament on the medial side of the elbow is replaced with a tendon from another part of a patient's body or from a cadaver.

Ultimate Fighting Championship (UFC): An American mixed martial arts promotion company.

Walk: Occurs when a pitcher throws four pitches out of the strike zone, none of which are swung at by the hitter.

Wins above replacement (WAR): Measures a player's value in all facets of the game by deciphering how many more wins he's worth than a replacement-level player at his same position.

WFAN: An all-day sports talk radio station licensed to New York City.

Wild Card: A team that did not win its division by the end of the regular season but has the best record among all non-division winners in the league.

Wild Card Era: A term that refers to the modern team alignments in each division, which began prior to the start of the 1994 season.

Wild Card Game: First round playoff matchup between the "Wild Card" winners in the AL and NL.

World Series: The annual championship series of Major League Baseball in North America, contested since 1903 between the American League champion team and the National League champion team.

Yankees.com: The official website of the New York Yankees.

Yankees Entertainment and Sports Network (YES): An American pay television regional sports network.

Yankee Stadium: A baseball park located in the Bronx, New York City, and home field for the New York Yankees.

Yankee Universe: An endearing term used to describe all matters related to Yankees baseball.

References

Books

Bashe, Philip. *Dog Days: The New York Yankees' Fall from Grace and Return to Glory, 1964–1976*. Random House, 1994.

Brown, Brené. *Dare to Lead: Brave Work. Tough Conversations. Whole Hearts*. Random House, 2018.

Fetter, Henry D. *Taking on the Yankees: Winning and Losing in the Business of Baseball*. W. W. Norton & Company, 2005.

Helyar, Jon. *Lords of the Realm: The Real History of Baseball*. Ballantine Books, 1995.

Hoch, Bryan. *The Baby Bombers: The Inside Story of the Next Yankees Dynasty*. Diversion Books, 2018.

Kernan, Kevin. *Girardi: Passion in Pinstripes*. Triumph Books, 2012.

Lewis, Michael. *Moneyball: The Art of Winning an Unfair Game*. W.W. Norton, 2004.

Lindbergh, Ben and Sam Miller. *The Only Rule Is It Has to Work: Our Wild Experiment Building a New Kind of Baseball Team*. Henry Holt and Company, 2016.

Lindbergh, Ben and Travis Sawchik. T*he MVP Machine: How Baseball's New Nonconformists Are Using Data to Build Better Players*. Basic Books, 2019.

Madden, Bill. *Steinbrenner: The Last Lion of Baseball*. Harper, 2010.

O'Connor, Ian. *The Captain: The Journey of Derek Jeter*. Mariner Books, 2012.

Olney, Buster. *The Last Night of the Yankee Dynasty: The Game, the Team, and the Cost of Greatness*. Harper Perennial, 2004.

Shalin, Mike. Donnie *Baseball: The Definitive Biography of Don Mattingly*. Triumph Books, 2011.

Solotaroff, Paul and Bob Klapisch. *Inside the Empire: The True Power Behind the New York Yankees.* Houghton Mifflin Harcourt, 2019.

Torre, Joe and Tom Verducci. *The Yankee Years.* Anchor, 2010.

Walker, Sam. *The Captain Class: The Hidden Force That Creates the World's Greatest Teams.* Random House, 2017.

Articles

Adler, Lindsey. "'Hey, Be Yourself': How the Yankees Embrace Scrappy..." *The Athletic*, 5 Aug. 2019, theathletic.com/1117317/2019/08/05/hey-be-yourself-how-the-yankees-embrace-scrappy-unknowns-who-have-sparked-their-season/.

Araton, Harvey. "Winfield and Steinbrenner and Reconciling the Past." *The New York Times*, 18 July 2008, https://www.nytimes.com/2008/07/18/sports/baseball/18araton.html.

Axisa, Mike. "On This Date in 1980: Dave Winfield Signs Richest Contract in Sports History." *CBSSports.com*, 15 Dec. 2015, www.cbssports.com/mlb/news/on-this-date-in-1980-dave-winfield-signs-richest-contract-in-sports-history/.

Axisa, Mike. "We Play Today, We Win Today, Das It: The Out of Nowhere Greatness of Mariano Duncan." *River Avenue Blues*, 3 Feb. 2016, riveraveblues.com/2016/02/we-play-today-we-win-today-das-it-the-out-of-nowhere-greatness-of-mariano-duncan-133005/.

Brown, Dave. "Jorge Posada Bitter toward Yankees Management in Book." *CBSSports.com*, 1 June 2015, www.cbssports.com/mlb/news/jorge-posada-bitter-toward-yankees-management-in-book/.

Brown, Maury. "MLB Sees Record Revenues of $10.3 Billion For 2018." *Forbes*, 7 Jan. 2019, www.forbes.com/sites/maurybrown/2019/01/07/mlb-sees-record-revenues-of-10-3-billion-for-2018/#f7f056d5beab.

Castellano, Anthony, and Michael Rothman. "How Baseball Helped New York Heal Post 9/11." *ABC News*, abcnews.go.com/US/fullpage/baseball-yankees-helped-york-heal-post-911-president-33663881.

Chass, Murray. "Thurman Munson Was Proud Captain of the Yankees." *The New York Times*, 3 Aug. 1979, www.nytimes.com/1979/08/03/archives/thurman-munson-was-proud-captain-of-the-yankees-his-family-most.html.

Coffey, Wayne. "Always the Captain: Consistency, Winning - and a Special Fan - Part of Derek Jeter's Legacy." *Nydailynews.com*, 7 Sept. 2014, www.nydailynews.com/sports/baseball/yankees/consistency-winning-special-fan-part-derek-jeter-legacy-article-1.1930295.

Drebinger, John. "61,808 Fans Roar Tribute to Gehrig", *The New York Times*, July 5, 1939.

Frollo, Joe. "Diana Munson Recalls the Softer Side of Steinbrenner." *The Repository*, 13 July 2010, www.cantonrep.com/article/20100713/NEWS/307139871.

Gardner, Sam. "How Aaron Judge Measures up to Other Historically Tall MLB Hitters." *FOX Sports*, 10 May 2017, www.foxsports.com/mlb/gallery/how-aaron-judge-measures-up-to-other-historically-tall-mlb-hitters-051017.

Giorgi, Hilary. "Yankees Magazine: The Ultimate Comeback." *MLB.com*, 11 Sept. 2018, www.mlb.com/yankees/news/baseball-helped-heal-the-nation-after-9-11-c294183722.

Golianopoulos, Thomas. "Yankees Magazine: Where Legends Live." *MLB.com*, 15 Dec. 2017, www.mlb.com/news/history-of-monument-park-c263612104.

Gonzalez, Roberto. "Neagle Still Miffed by Early Lift." *Courant.com*, 27 Oct. 2000, www.courant.com/news/connecticut/hc-xpm-2000-10-27-0010270516-story.html.

Hu, Winnie. "A Public Park to Rival the Yankees' Playground." *The New York Times*, 5 Apr. 2012, www.nytimes.com/2012/04/06/nyregion/heritage-field-opens-near-yankee-stadium.html.

Kuty, Brendan. "Hero of the Day: How the Yankees Pick Who Gets Their Championship Belt after Wins." *Nj.com*, 22 May 2019,

www.nj.com/yankees/2019/05/how-the-yankees-pick-who-gets-
their-championship-belt.html.

Lupica, Mike. "Lemon Will Be Remembered for Yankees Summer
of '78." *Los Angeles Times*, 16 Jan. 2000, www.latimes.com/archives/la-
xpm-2000-jan-16-sp-54493-story.html.

Madden, Bill. "Johnny Damon Feels Joe Torre's Book Is Just Not
Write about 2007 Season." *Nydailynews.com*, 1 Mar. 2009,
www.nydailynews.com/sports/baseball/yankees/johnny-damon-feels-
joe-torre-book-not-write-2007-season-article-1.365828.

Marchand, Andrew. "Is Joe Girardi Having Fun Yet?" *ABC7 New
York*, 10 Mar. 2017, abc7ny.com/sports/is-joe-girardi-having-fun-
yet/1794120/.

McCarron, Anthony. "Joe Torre and the Spirit of '96: From
'Clueless Joe' to Beginning of a Dynasty, a Q&A with the Yankees
Skipper." *Nydailynews.com*, 14 Aug. 2016,
www.nydailynews.com/sports/baseball/yankees/joe-torre-spirit-96-q-
yankee-skipper-article-1.2749827.

Mittler, Doug. "Everything You Need to Know about the 2018
Season's New Managers." *ESPN*, 9 Feb. 2018,
www.espn.com/mlb/story/_/id/22383673/everything-need-know-
2018-season-new-managers.

Naughton, Jim. "Yankees' Thurman Munson Killed Piloting His
Own Small Jet in Ohio." *The New York Times*, 3 Aug. 1979,
www.nytimes.com/1979/08/03/archives/yankees-thurman-munson-
killed-piloting-his-own-small-jet-in-ohio.html.

O'Connor, Ian. "Bernie Williams a Yankee of Uncommon Dignity,
Grace." *ESPN*, 21 May 2015,
www.espn.com/mlb/story/_/id/12926321/new-york-yankees-bernie-
williams-uncommon-dignity-grace.

Pennington, Bill. "Billy's Biggest Brawl." *Sports Illustrated*,
www.si.com/longform/2015/1985/billy-martin/index.html.

Pepe, Phil. "Reggie Jackson and Billy Martin Clash in Fenway Park
Dugout in 1977." *Nydailynews.com*, 8 Apr. 2018,
www.nydailynews.com/sports/baseball/yankees/reggie-jackson-billy-
martin-brawl-fenway-park-1977-article-1.2673731.

Ryan, Liz. "Five Signs Your CEO Is Incompetent." *Forbes*, 9 Mar. 2015, www.forbes.com/sites/lizryan/2015/03/08/five-signs-your-ceo-is-incompetent/#5d3f6738.

Shafer, Jacob. "Is 2009 or 2014 Spending Spree More to Blame for Yankees' Payroll Mess?" *Bleacher Report*, 26 May 2016, bleacherreport.com/articles/2642348-is-2009-or-2014-spending-spree-more-to-blame-for-yankees-payroll-mess.

"Torre Turns Down Offer to Return as Yanks' Skipper." *ESPN*, 18 Oct. 2007, www.espn.com/mlb/news/story?id=3069115.

"Tour The New Yankees Stadium." *Nydailynews.com*, web.archive.org/web/20090405003627/http://www.nydailynews.com/sports/baseball/yankees/yankeestadium/index.html.

Websites

www.baseball-reference.com
www.mlb.com
www.silvershieldfoundation.org
www.yankees.com

Film

1996 World Series - New York Yankees vs Atlanta Braves. VHS. Directed by Rich Domich. Secaucus, NJ: Major League Baseball Productions, 1996.

Tweets

Grant, Adam. Twitter Post. July 18, 2018, 8:05 AM. https://twitter.com/AdamMGrant/status/1019553743333969926.

Feinsand, Mark. Twitter Post. July 31, 2016, 10:49 AM. https://twitter.com/Feinsand/status/759762952979378176.

About the Author

Colin Cerniglia is the founder and CEO of the Talent 409 Leadership Academy. The Talent 409 Leadership Academy works with athletes and coaches to guide them through their leadership development. The Leadership Academy also works with athletic teams to enhance their vision and culture.

Colin is also the creator and host of the *Dynamic Leaders Podcast*. The podcast is a weekly show featuring some of the most compelling leaders in sports and in business. These guests share their stories while providing tips and tools for listeners to become better leaders.

For more about the Talent 409 Leadership Academy, or the *Dynamic Leaders Podcast*, please visit www.talent409.com.

Photo: Hailey Kemper/Wildflower Photography

Colin lives in Charlotte, North Carolina, with his wife, Christine, and his daughter, Stella.